D1459635

**THIS IS A BORZOI BOOK
PUBLISHED BY
ALFRED A. KNOPF**

Copyright © 1998 Alfred
A. Knopf, New York

All rights reserved under
International and Pan-American
Copyright Conventions. Published
in the United States by
Alfred A. Knopf, a division of
Random House, Inc., New York,
and simultaneously in Canada by
Random House of Canada
Limited, Toronto. Distributed by
Random House, Inc., New York.

www.aaknopf.com

Knopf, Borzoi Books, and the
colophon are registered
trademarks of Random House, Inc.

ISBN 0-375-70611-9
Library of Congress number
98-87663

First published May 1999
Revised and updated April 2001

Originally published in France by
Nouveaux Loisirs, a subsidiary of
Gallimard, Paris 1998, and in Italy by
Touring Editore, Srl., Milano 1998.
Copyright © 1998 Nouveaux
Loisirs, Touring Editore, Srl.

SERIES EDITORS
Seymourina Cruse/Marisa Bassi
RIO EDITION: Mélanie Le Bris, Amandine
Galopin, Seymourina Cruse
GRAPHICS Élizabeth Cohat and
Yann Le Duc
LAYOUT: Gérard Dumas and Olivier
Lauga
MINI-MAPS, MAPS OF THE AREA:
Kristoff Chemineau
STREET MAPS: Touring Club Italiano
PRODUCTION Catherine Bourrabier

Translated by Simon Knight and typeset by
The Write Idea in association with First
Edition Translations Ltd, Cambridge, UK

Printed in Italy by
Editoriale Lloyd

Authors
RIO DE JANEIRO

Romaric Sulger Büel (1)
When he worked for the AFAA
(Association française d'action artistique),
R. Sulger Büel traveled the world organizing
art exhibitions. As cultural attaché in Rio
from 1993 to 1998, he fell in love with the
city, of which he has an encyclopaedic
knowledge. We are very grateful for his help
in producing and proofreading this guide.

Things you need to know:
Théodore Fleury (2)
With a French mother and Carioca father,
Th. Fleury has lived all his life in Rio, while
making regular trips to Europe. This has
given him a comprehensive understanding
of everything the visitor will need to know
when arriving and spending time in this city.

Where to stay and **After dark:**
Vincent Brochier (3)
V. Brochier arrived in Rio in 1994 for a
period of voluntary service, and was in
charge of the French embassy's book
department. A tireless reveler, he has an
unrivaled knowledge of Rio's nightlife.

What to see and **Further afield:**
Jean-François Chougnet (4)
A historian by training, J.-F. Chougnet soon
developed a special interest in the
Portuguese-speaking world. After doing
various jobs in Lisbon, he made a special
study of the history of Rio during the
Napoleonic era, when it was temporarily
the Portuguese capital.

What to see and **Further afield:**
Bertrand Rigot-Müller (5)
Having studied economics, B. Rigot-Müller
went to Brazil in 1968 to work for a year
as a demographer. Irresistibly attracted to
that country, he settled in Rio, where for
the last thirty years he has taken part in the
city's cultural life and organized numerous
cultural events.

Where to eat and **Where to
shop:** Manuèle Colas (6)
Originally from Paris, M. Colas has lived in
Rio for almost ten years. She imports a
number of French products, keeping a close
watch on developments in the local market.
Her enthusiasm for the local cuisine means
she is always on the look-out for new
restaurants, and happy to share her discoveries.

Things you need to know ➡6

Where to stay ➡16

Where to eat ➡30

After dark ➡48

What to see ➡62

Further afield ➡88

Where to shop ➡100

Finding your way ➡114

Symbols

☎ telephone
⇛ fax
● price or price range
🕐 opening hours
▤ credit cards accepted
🗗 credit cards not accepted
🔽 toll-free number
@ e-mail/website address
★ tips and recommendations

Access

Ⓜ subway stations
🚌 bus (or tram)
🅿 private parking
🅿 parking attendant
♿ no facilities for the disabled
🚆 train
🚗 car
🚢 boat

Hotels

☎ telephone in room
📠 fax in room on request
🍸 minibar
📺 television in room
❄ air-conditioned rooms
🕐 24-hour room service
🛎 caretaker
👶 babysitting
🏢 meeting room(s)
🐾 no pets
🍳 breakfast
☕ open for tea/coffee
🍴 restaurant
🎵 live music
💿 disco
🌳 garden, patio or terrace
🏋 gym, fitness club
🏊 swimming pool, sauna

Restaurants

🥗 vegetarian food
🏞 view
👔 formal dress required
🚬 smoking area
🍸 bar

Museums and galleries

🏬 on-site store(s)
👁 guided tours
☕ café

Stores

🔀 branches, outlets

The Insider's Guide is made up of **8 sections** each indicated by a different color.

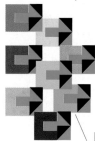

Things you need to know (mauve)
Where to stay (blue)
Where to eat (red)
After dark (pink)
What to see (green)
Further afield (orange)
Where to shop (yellow)
Finding your way (purple)

Where to stay

In the area
Ipanema is of course well known as the cradle of the bossa-nova. However, it is a lively district with many businesses and restaurants. The sun rises on the Arpoador (Copacabana direction) and sets behind the mountains of the Two brothers (Dois Irmãos), on whose slopes is the favela of Vidigal.

Caesar Park (14)
Avenida Vieira Souto, 460 - Ipanema ☎ 525 25 25 ⇛ 521 60 00

Sol Ipanema (15)
Avenida Vieira Souto, 320 - Ipanema ☎ 523 00 95 ⇛ 521 64

Everest Rio (16)
Rua Prudente de Morais, 1117 - Ipanema ☎ 523 22 82 ⇛ 521 31

Country Residence Service (17)
Rua Prudente de Morais, 1706 - Ipanema ☎ 511 52 52 ⇛ 259 09

Not forgetting
■ **Monsieur Le Blond (18)** Avenida Bartolomeu Mitre, 455 - Leblon
■ **Praia Ipanema (19)** Avenida Vieira Souto, 706 - Ipanema
■ **Arpoador Inn (20)** Rua Francisco Otaviano, 177 - Ipanema

Practical information
is given for each particular establishment: opening times, prices, ways of paying, different services available

How to use this guide

The section **"In the area"** refers you (➡ 00) to other establishments that are covered in a different section of the guide but found in the same area of the city.

In the area

Ipanema is, of course, well known as it is a lively district with many busine

■ Where to eat ➡ 34
■ After dark ➡ 50 ➡ 5ː
➡ 56 ■ Where to shoｐ

Ipanema / Leblon **D** D1-4

nícius de Moraes
5
3   8   4 21
40
Joana Angélica

The small map
shows all the
establishments
mentioned and others
described elsewhere but
found "in the area", by
the color of the section.

**The name of the
district** is given
above the map. A grid
reference (**A** B-C 2)
enables you to find it in
the section on Maps at
the end of the book.

This luxury apartment hotel stands oｐ
Club. ★ The individual apartments are

Hot tips, indicated by a star ★, contains advice
from the author: the best rooms, recommended
dishes, views not to be missed…

Not forgetting

■ **Monsieur Le Blond (18)** Aveni
☎ 539 30 30 ➡ 529 32 20 ●● *Good qualiː*

The section "Not forgetting"
lists other useful addresses in the same area..

The opening page
to each section
contains an index
ordered alphabetically
(Getting there),
by subject or
by district (After dark)
as well as useful
addresses and advice.

**The section
"Things you need
to know"** covers
information on getting
to Rio and day-to-day
life in the city.

Theme pages
introduce a selection
of establishments on
a given topic.

**The "Maps"
section** of this guide
contains 6 street plans
of Rio followed by
a detailed index.

Useful website from the USA
www.brazilny.org
Useful website from the UK
www.brazil.org.uk

Getting there

Electricity supply

Everywhere in Rio, the power supply is 127 V (60 Hz), from two-pin sockets. Hotels provide adaptors for the use of their clients.

Time difference

Rio is 3 hours behind GMT. At midday in Rio, it is 3pm in London and 10am in New York. However, when the clocks change in March and October the time difference will be an hour greater or smaller.

Formalities

Visitors will need a return ticket, and a passport valid for 6 months after their planned date of return. American and Canadian citizens require a visa. If you intend to stay for more than 90 days, report to the federal police within 60 days of arrival. Recommended vaccinations: yellow fever, polio, typhoid, hepatitis A and B.

40
Things
you need to Know

Brazilian consulate in New York

1185 Avenue of the Americas, 21st floor, New York 10036
☎ 212 827 0976 ➡ (212) 827 0225
Mon.–Fri. 10am–4pm (for Brazilian residents only)
Mon.–Fri. 10am–noon; 1–3pm (for US citizens)

Brazilian embassy in London

32 Green Street, London W1Y 4AT
Mon.–Fri. 10am–1pm, 3–6pm
☎ 020 7499 0877 ➡ 020 7399 9100
@ infolondres@infolondres.org.uk

National holidays

Jan. 1 New Year
Jan. 20 Festival of São Sebastião (Rio's patron saint)
Sat. to Ash Wednesday Carnival carioca (➡ 60)
Mar.–Apr Paixão (Good Friday); Páscoa (Easter Day)
Apr. 21 Celebration in honor of Tiradentes (martyr of independence)
May 1 Festa do Trabalho (Labor Day)
May Ascensão (Ascension Day); Espírito Santo (Whitsun)
June Festas Juninas (Saint Anthony, Saint John, Saint Peter)
Sep. 7 Independence Day
Oct. 12 Nossa Senhora de Aparechida (patron saint of Brazil)
Nov. 2 Finados (All Souls' Day)
Nov. 15 Proclamation of the Republic (and the day elections are held)
Dec. 25 Christmas

INDEX A–Z

Rio de Janeiro is served by two airports: Galeão (pronounced "gal-y-on") international airport, approximately 9 miles from the city center, and Santos Dumont airport, right in town, which is used for regional flights. Both airports are built on the bay, so you can be sure of a spectacular approach.

Arriving

Galeão-Tom Jobim (1)

International airport in the northern part of the city, on Governador island. Arrivals at ground level.
● airport tax R$36 payable in cash (dollars or reais)

Information
☎ 398 41 33/34

Lost property
☎ 398 41 52

Car rental
Ground floor
Hertz
☎ 398 43 38
🕒 Daily, 24 hours
Mega
☎ 398 33 57
🕒 Daily 6am–midnight
Localiza
☎ 398 54 45
🕒 Daily 6am–midnight

Taxis
Choose taxis for which you pay

prior to departure (*Transcoopass*, red, or *Cootramo*, blue) at the window in the arrivals area of the airport concourse.
● airport–town center R$ 28

Money
Travelers' checks and foreign currency can be changed at the Banco do Brasil agency. You can also withdraw money from cash dispensers: Bradesco, Banco 24 horas and Itaú on the 3rd floor.

Duty free
Better facilities on arrival than on departure.
☎ 398 39 26
or 398 44 23
● you are allowed to bring in goods worth US$ 500

Telephone
Phone cards are on sale at the office of *Telemar* (local telecoms company) on the 3rd floor.
☎ 398 59 75
or 398 37 39
🕒 Daily, 24 hours
Payment accepted in reais or in dollars

Post office (Correios)
3rd floor
☎ 503 83 33
🕒 Mon.–Sat. 7am–8pm

Galeão/Santos Dumont shuttle
The Real company minibus stops en route at the Novo Rio bus station and the Praça Mauá.
● R$ 2.50
🕒 Daily 7am–9pm Departures every 20 mins

Line 2018 goes to Barra da Tijuca, calling at the Novo Rio bus station, Praça Mauá, Santos Dumont airport and the beaches.
● R$ 5
🕒 Daily 5.30am–11pm. Departures every 30 mins

Santos Dumont (2)

National airport in the carioca business district. Starting point of the aerial bridges toward Brasília, Belo Horizonte and São Paulo.

Aerial link Rio–São Paulo
The journey between Rio and São Paulo is easier via the national airport than the international ones which are far from the city center (be

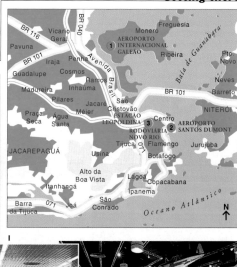

aware of this when buying your tickets). Boarding in the national airport is fast, simple and usually doesn't require any booking.
🔲 *Departure every 30 mins (every 10 mins during peak hours). Journey 45 mins.*
● *airport tax R$ 7.20-9.15 payable in cash*

Information
☎ 814 72 24/46

Car rental
Hertz
☎ 262 06 12
🔲 *Daily 6am–11pm*
Mega
☎ 262 36 17
🔲 *Daily 6am–11pm*
Localiza
☎ 220 54 55
🔲 *Daily 6am–midnight*

Taxis
Taxis can be hired

outside the airport.

Money
There are no exchange facilities in this airport. Money can be withdrawn from cash dispensers: Bradesco, Banco 24 horas and Itaú.

Telephones
Telemar
🔲 *Daily 6am–10.30pm*

Post office (Correios)
🔲 *Mon.–Fri. 9am–5pm, mail collected 3.35pm*

Bus
The stop is opposite the airport entrance; the Real company operates two lines serving Barra da Tijuca, Galeão and the city center.

Hotels
Aeroporto Othon
➥ 24

Bus services (3)
In Brazil one does not travel by train but by bus. It is the most popular and cheapest form of transportation, with rapid services to all Brazil's major cities. For greater comfort, choose a bus with air-conditioning or couchettes (*leito*). Tickets purchased at travel agencies cost R$ 1.20 more than those bought at the bus terminal.

Rodoviária Novo Rio bus station
Av. Francisco Bicalho, 1 - Santo Cristo
☎ 291 51 51
Dantur assagens e Turismo Agency
Av. Rio Branco, basement , 156 (Loja 134) - Centro

☎ 262 34 24
or 262 36 24

Car travel
Three main roads converge on Rio. The **BR-116** (or Via Dutra) from São Paolo, and the **BR-040** from Petrópolis, Belo Horizonte and Brasília, bring you into the Linha Vermelha or the Avenida Brasil. The **BR-101** arrives at the Rio-Niterói bridge, if you are coming from the north, or the Avenida Brasil and Barra da Tijuca, if you are coming from the south (Angra and Paraty).
● *tolls BR-116 R$ 3.50; BR-040 R$ 3; BR-101 R$ 1.40 as you leave on the Rio Niterói*

Buses run at all hours of the day and night, though services are less frequent between 11pm and 6am. To travel by bus, you need to be familiar with the various districts and the routes operated by the private bus companies, which can be recognized by their livery. Cariocas tend to use taxis, especially at night. Take care when on foot: the traffic is fast-

→ Getting around

Buses

The most popular means of transport, though route plans are complicated and the buses have no air-conditioning.

Routes

Several companies may cover the same route, and stops are irregular. The *circulares* circle round all the Zona Sul, and start from the following districts (make sure you are going in the right direction): Urca (511 and 512) Glória (571) and Laranjeiras (573 and 574) and Cosme Velho (583 and 584).

Tips

• Do not carry valuables such as cameras and wristwatches.

• The entrance is at the back.
• There are no tickets: you pay as you go through the turnstile inside the bus.
• Route numbers and the main stops may be displayed on the new bus stops.
● R$ 0.70
On some routes there are more expensive air-conditioned services (*frescão*).

Cultural tour

With this pass (valid for one day) you can use the special bus that links the main museums in the city center: Museu de Arte Moderna, Museu de Belas Artes, Museu Histórico etc.
Information
☎ 533 44 07

◐ Tue.–Sun.
11.30am–7.30pm
*Departs every
30 mins in front of
the Paço Imperial*
➡ 66.   ● R$ 3

Subway

Safe and clean. Its two lines cover the center and northern areas of the city. For the south, beyond Copacabana, take a bus. The carriages have air-conditioning.
Information
☎ 296 61 16
◐ Mon.–Sat.
6am–11pm
● Mon.–Fri.
noon–4pm,
8–11pm; Sat. and
public hol R$ 0.80;
Mon.–Fri. 6am–
noon, 4–8pm R$1

Taxis

The most practical form of transport in

town. The regular yellow taxis, with a blue band along the side, can be hailed anywhere. Other taxis, of various colors, are 20% dearer but are air-conditioned and more comfortable. At bus stations and airports, the taxi companies offer fixed fares, depending on your destination, which you pay at the office prior to departure. It is worth paying more to avoid the risk of an unpleasant scene when it comes to paying the driver. For taxis with meters, the fare displayed is fully inclusive: do not pay any more:
● *tariff 1 Mon.–Sat.
6am–9pm*

moving and stops
for no one!

● *tariff 2 (in the
suburbs and on
the coast)
Jan.–Nov.: Mon.–
Sat. 9pm–6am;
Sun. and Dec.:
24 hours*
● *supplement
for bulky luggage
R$ 1.20*
**Central de Táxi
(yellow)**
☎ 593 25 98
**Coopertramo
(white)**
☎ 560 20 22

Cycling

Rio has 45 miles
of cycle track.
For instance, it is
easy to get from
Leblon to the
city center via
the beaches ➡ 80
and the Flamengo
gardens ➡ 72.
In summer, you
can rent a bicycle
from itinerant
dealers along
the Lagoa and
at Ipanema.

● *R$ 5 / hour*

Streetcars

The only
remaining stretch
of the old street-
car network
(*Bonde*) runs from
the city center to
Santa Tereza. It
leaves from the
foot of the
Petrobrás tower,
runs along the
top of the Arcos
de Lapa ➡ 76, and
has two separate
termini at Santa
Tereza: Dois
Irmãos and
Largo das Neves.
A splendid way
to view the city.
🕐 *Daily 6am–
11pm, does not
run in heavy rain*
● *R$ 0.65*

Barcas

Ferries which ply
between Rio and
Niterói ➡84 and
between Rio and
Paquetá island

➡ 84. The landing
stage is at the
Praça XV.
● *Niterói: R$ 0.90
Paquetá:
Mon.–Fri. R$ 1.10;
Sat.–Sun. R$ 2.25*

Cars

Poor road signs,
the speed and
unpredictability
of the traffic, and
parking difficulties
make it hard to
get around by car,
except in the São
Conrado and
Barra districts.

Car rental
Agencies are
mainly at the
airports and at
Copacabana,
on the Avenida
Princesa Isabel.

Parking
Whether in an
official car park
or not, it is wise
to pay R$ 1 or 2
to the person
watching over
your car.

Fuel

Readily available,
and cheaper than
in the UK but
dearer than in the
US: some vehicles
run on alcohol, so
make sure you fill
up at the right
pump.

Helicopters

Increasingly used
by businessmen,
though still
expensive.
Departures
from heliports
at the Lagoa, the
Corcovado ➡ 84
(Mirante Dona
Marta) and the
Sugar Loaf ➡ 84
(intermediate
port of call).
Hélisight
*Rua Visconde de
Pirajá, 580 -
Ipanema*
☎ 511 21 41
● *R$ 65 for
7 mins, 4 pers.
maximum.*

Security has greatly improved in recent years. It is nevertheless wise to observe certain rules: leave passports, jewelry and money in the hotel safe, and only carry the bare essentials. At many places in town, visitors can obtain information from the interactive terminals installed by the municipality.

Getting by

VAGA CERTA
PERÍODO ÚNICO
R$ 2,00

Tourism

British consulate
Praia do Flamengo 284/2 Andar
☎ 553 55 07
🔲 Mon.–Fri. 8.30am–5pm

American consulate
Avenida Presidente Wilson, 147
☎ 292 7117
www.consulado-americano-rio.org

Riotur (2)
Rua da Assembléia, 10 (10th floor) - Centro
☎ 217 75 75
🔲 Mon.–Fri. 9am–6pm
Tourist office.

Money

Currency
Since July 1994, the unit of currency has been the real (R$), worth roughly 30p/48c, which is divided into 100 centavos.

There are 1, 5, 10, 50 and 100 real notes, and coins worth 1, 5, 10, 25 and 50 centavos, and 1 real.

Banks
Most banks have cash dispensers, but Visa cards are accepted only by some Bradesco dispensers and at certain Banco do Brasil outlets. MasterCard and Diners' Club cards are accepted by outlets of the Itaú bank.
🔲 Mon.–Fri. 10am–4pm

Credit cards
Widely accepted, except in some restaurants. Be warned: if you come across the old system of payment, destroy the carbon copy to avoid the risk of counterfeiting.

If your cards are lost or stolen
Am. Express
☎ 0800 78 50 50
MasterCard / Diners Club
☎ 0800 78 44 44 (220 90 90 after 8pm)
Visa
☎ 292 53 54

Bureaux de change
The best place to change money is at a casa de câmbio (bureau de change), which will offer a better rate than a bank. Hotels also tend to take a higher commission. The American dollar is accepted in some hotels and shops, and is by far the easiest currency to change. Dollar travelers' checks are widely accepted, but

there is a 1% commission on transactions.

Casas de câmbio
Irmãos Cupello, Av. Rio Branco, 31-A - Centro
☎ 233 56 75
Casa Universal Câmbio Viagens e Turismo, Av. N.S. de Copacabana, 371, (Lj. E) - Copacabana
☎ 548 66 96

Telephone

Public telephones
Called orelhão (big ears) on account of their shape, public telephone booths are operated by cards, which can be bought from post offices and Telemar stores (local telecoms company), or at news-stands.

Dialing codes
Calling Rio from the UK:

12

00 55 21 + local number;
from the US:
011 55 21 + local number.
Calling abroad from Rio: 00 + country code + regional code (without the 0) + local number.
Calling Rio from other parts of Brasil: 021 + local number.

Collect calls
Within Brazil
9 + regional code
Within Rio
9 + 021 + number
When calling abroad
000 111, then wait for the operator

Useful numbers
Directory inquiries
☎ 102
Lost property (4)
Rua 1° de Março,

64 - Centro
☎ 159

Mail
Postage stamps are sold only at post offices, so it is best to visit a post office when sending a letter.
Central post office (4)
Av. Presidente Vargas, 3077 - Centro
☎ 503 82 22
🕐 Mon.–Fri. 9am–5pm

Media
Local newspapers
Dailies published in Rio: O Globo; Jornal do Brasil; O Dia; Gazeta Mercantil (financial affairs).
Good weekly supplements on Fridays in the Globo (Rio Show) and in the Jornal do Brasil (Programa)

giving details of all the weekend's cultural activities.
Weeklies: Veja (with cultural supplement Veja-Rio), Isto É, Exame (the economy).
International newspapers
On sale at large news-stands in the Zona Sul (Ipanema, Copacabana, Leblon), the city center, and at Letras & Expressões
➡ 104.

Television
There are 4 major national commercial channels (Globo, SBT, Manchete and Bandeirantes), a public-service cultural channel (TV Educativa) and two main cable operators: TVA and NET.

Health matters
Emergency services
Police
☎ 190
Fire, ambulance
☎ 193
Hospital (free)
Miguel Couto
Av. Bartolomeu Mitre, 1108 - Leblon
☎ 274 60 50
Emergencies
☎ 274 21 21
Clinic
Clinica São Vicente
Rua Joao Borges 204 - Gávea
☎ 529 44 22
Pharmacies (24 hours)
Farmácia Piauí
Av. Ataúlfo de Paiva, 1283-A - Leblon
☎ 274 73 22
Drogaria Colombo
Rua Visconde de Pirajá, 499-A - Ipanema
☎ 511 35 21

Basic facts

Rio is magnificently situated between sea and mountains, providing an ideal setting for most open-air sports: forest walks ➡ 84, climbing on the morros, water sports on lagoon and open sea, beach activities, parascending, and delta-planing around the mountain tops.

➡ Getting fit

Sports in Rio

Soccer (1)
Cariocas have soccer in their blood. A game on the beach or a big match at the Maracanã stadium ➡ 86 is always an exciting show. Tickets for the Maracanã go on sale a week before the match at club grounds, and at the stadium's own ticket office. You have a choice between a place on the terraces (*arquibancada*), if you want to share the emotion of the fans, or a seat (*cadeira*) in the stands.
● *arquibancada and cadeira R$ 6–10*
● *cadeira especial R$ 30–50*
● *club sweaters on sale in sports shops R$ 40*

Beach sports
Various sports are practiced on Rio's beaches, but divers and swimmers should take care: the sea is sometimes polluted and dangerous. However, the beaches of Barra da Tijuca, Prainha and Grumarí ➡ 80 are always clean.

Futevôlei
Played mainly on the beaches of Ipanema and Copacabana. The pitch and rules are the same as for beach volleyball, but the ball is played with the feet.

Beach volleyball
This very popular game is played by both men and women on the beaches of Ipanema, Barra da Tijuca and Copacabana.

Surfing (2)
Rio is not Hawaii, but the Atlantic waves offer plenty of excitement. The best spots are at Prainha and Grumarí.
*Surf boards
Rua F. Otaviano, 67 - Arpoador
☎ 522 87 27*
🕓 *Mon.–Fri. 10am–7pm; Sat. 9am–5pm*
● *Hire of boards R$ 20 per day*

Frescoball
A common sight in Rio, this is the beach version of badminton, played in shallow water with wooden rackets and a rubber ball.
● *a pair of rackets R$ 20*

Jet-skiing
Jet-skis can be hired at Barra da Tijuca.
*Jet Park
Estrada da Barra da Tijuca, 253 - Barra da Tijuca*
● *R$45 for 30 mins*

Capoeira
A form of wrestling disguised as a dance, once practiced by the African slaves of Bahia and now very much in fashion. It is a great spectacle, performed to the rhythm of chants and percussion instruments, including the *berimbau*, under the watchful eye of the *mestre* (master).
Courses organized at the PUC

university, Rua
Marquês de São
Vicente, 225 -
Gávea
Mestre Garrincha
⊙ Wed.–Thurs.
Mon. 8–9.30pm
● R$ 10 / session

Deltaplane (3)
Superb double
flights in a
deltaplane can be
made from the
Pedra Bonita
take-off point,
landing on the
beach at São
Conrado ➡ 80.
Or you can try
parascending.
There are many
instructors willing
to accompany
you.
Superfly
☎ 322 22 86
or 99 82 57 03
● *transport to the
take-off point
R$ 80;*
● *with 12 photos
during the flight
R$ 100*

Rambling (4)
In the forest of
Tijuca ➡ 82, there
are several well-
defined paths,
though they are
not way-marked.
Take a guide to
show you the
many *cachoeiras*
(water fall).
*Centro
Excursionista
Brasileiro*
☎ 252 13 48 or
252 98 44

Rock-climbing (5)
There are many
rock-faces to
climb, particularly
in the vicinity of
the Sugar Loaf
➡ 84, and there
are a number of
prepared routes.

Golf (6)
Though golf is not
a Brazilian
tradition, you can
still play the game
on a magnificent

course between
sea and mountain.
Priority is given
to members and
their guests.
*Gávea Golf Club
Estrada da Gávea,
800 - São Conrado*
☎ 322 41 41
● *entrance fee
R$ 100*

Jogging (7)
A popular way
of keeping fit.
Cariocas run
on the *calçadão*
(beach-side side-
walk), or along
the Lagoa Rodrigo
de Freitas.
A marathon is
organized every
spring.

Carnival
It is often said
that in Brazil,
especially in Rio,
the year does not
begin until after
Carnival. A major
event for the
locals, it is always

held in the week
of Shrove Tuesday,
from the previous
Saturday until the
morning of Ash
Wednesday,
and includes a
traditional parade
put on by the
18 samba schools.
The winners of
the competition
also parade the
following week
end. Seats in the
Sambódromo (8)
➡ 60 are sold
several months in
advance (starting
the previous
October).
Ticket outlets are
announced each
year by Riotur.
The best seats are
in sectors 5, 7, 9
and 11, nearest
to the *baterias.*
● *Special group
(Sun.–Mon.)
R$ 10–180;
champions' parade
(following Sat.)
R$ 5-90.*

Brazilian motels
Unlike their counterparts in North America, motels in Rio are generally on the outskirts of the city and are used for amorous encounters ...

➡ Where to stay

Hotel services
Most hotels are concentrated in the Zona Sul. Apart from some expensive luxury hotels, most offer a very uniform standard of service. Do not go looking for old-world charm, it does not exist in Rio. For a warm welcome in a delightful setting, visit **Búzios** ➡ 92 and try the **Relais La Borie**, *Rua das Gravatás, 1374 - Praia de Geribá* ☎ *(024) 623 14 98*

Prices

The following information is given for each hotel: number of rooms and suites; price range of a double room; services provided. Please note that the prices given here do not include taxes (10 % service charge, 5 % service tax, and sometimes 1 % tourist tax).

46
Hotels

THE INSIDER'S FAVORITES

The Sheraton and the Inter-Continental

In this guide are listed hotels situated in downtown Rio, near the main beaches (Copacabana, Ipanema, Leblon), and in towns suggested for excursions. However, let's not forget two of the largest hotels in the Zona Sul:

The Sheraton Rio Hotel & Towers Avenida Niemeyer, 121 - Praia do Vidigal ☎ 274 11 22 ➡ 239 56 43
The Inter-Continental Rio Avenida Pref. Mendes de Morais, 222 - Praia de São Conrado ☎ 322 22 00 ➡ 322 55 00

INDEX BY PRICE

Basic facts

Copacabana, with the famous Avenida Atlântica, familiar from a million picture postcards, is virtually synonymous with Rio. The district, with its high-rise buildings often proves a disappointment, but for those with a discerning eye, it is still a magical place. Leme, between the Hotel

➡ Where to stay

Copacabana Palace (1)
Avenida Atlântica, 1702 - Copacabana ☎ 548 70 70 ➡ 235 73 30

[icons] **223 rooms** ●●●●● *127 suites R$ 495* *free for residents* [icons] Pergula, Cipriani ➡ *40* [icons] 0800 211 533 @ coparj@ibm.net

Try to imagine this palace when it was first built, in 1923. An isolated resort hotel, its guests then included the cream of Rio society and such famous visitors as the Queen of England, General de Gaulle, Edith Piaf and Orson Welles. Dignified and imposing, it was built in a neo-Louis XVI style by the French architect Joseph Gire. Nearly closed down in the early 1990s, the hotel was acquired in extremis by the Sherwood group and restored to its former glory. The entrance hall is strangely small, without the pomp and circumstance you would expect of such a place. The rooms are comfortable, and some offer a magnificent view of the beach. Its fine pool, once a fashionable rendezvous, is still a smart place to come and have breakfast. Reception rooms can be hired for society weddings, in particular the Golden Room, which was once used as a theater.

Grandville Ouro Verde (2)
Avenida Atlântica, 1546 - Copacabana ☎ 543 41 23 ➡ 542 45 97

[icons] *extra charge* [icons] **62 rooms** ●●● *2 suites R$ 240* [icons] Ouro Verde [icons] @ www.granville.com.br

Opened in 1952, this suberb, highly traditional hotel was under Swiss management until acquired recently by the Brazilian Grandville chain. The new owners have done a lot to enhance the reputation of the hotel, which is one of the most appealing in town, with rooms laid out around an impressive central courtyard. ★ Before venturing into the restaurant, once frequented by carioca high society, enjoy an aperitif on the attractive terrace overlooking the beach.

Le Méridien Copacabana (3)
Avenida Atlântica, 1020 - Leme ☎ 275 99 22 ➡ 541 64 47

[icons] **496 rooms** ●●●● *54 suites US$ 350* [icons] *on request* [icons] Le Saint-Honoré ➡ *40*, Le Café de la Paix [icons] Rond-Point [icons] @ sales@meridien-br.com

This was for many years the inevitable port of call of Air France crews and French politicians visiting Rio de Janeiro. The airline's disposal of the Méridien hotel chain has been followed by a refurbishment, which is obvious the moment you enter the hotel lobby. ★ Ask for a room on one of the upper floors. The Saint-Honoré ➡ *40*, supervised by top French chef Paul Bocuse, is one of Rio's most highly regarded restaurants.

Not forgetting

■ **Rio International Hotel (4)** Avenida Atlântica, 1500 - Copacabana ☎ 543 15 55 ➡ 542 54 43 ●●●● *Classic hotel, with a magnificent view.*
■ **Real Palace Hotel (5)** Rua Duvivier, 70 - Copacabana ☎ 541 43 87 ➡ 542 23 98 ●●● *If you want to stay in Copacabana town.*
■ **Leme Othon Palace (6)** Avenida Atlântica, 656 - Leme ☎ ➡ 543 80 80 ●●● *The Leme offers tranquility, on a pleasant stretch of the beach.*

Méridien and the Morro do Leme, has retained its peace and charm.

■ Where to eat ➡ 40

6

1

1

3

In the area

The second half of the beach runs as far as the fort. It is frequented, day and night, by joggers, footballers, surfers, swimmers and insomniacs. From lookout post 6, there is a view of the beach, with the Sugar Loaf in the background ➡ 84 and the other *morros* at the entrance to the bay.

Where to stay

Hotel Sofitel Rio Palace (7)
Avenida Atlântica, 4240 - Copacabana ☎ 525 12 32 ➡ 525 12 30

M **P** ***388 rooms*** ●●●●● *32 suites R$ 350* 🔲 🔲 🔲 🔲 🔲 🔲 🔲 🔲 🔲
Atlantis 🔲 *Lobby Bar, Rorce Neck Bar* 🔲 🔲 🔲 🔲 🔲 🔲 🔲 🔲 *(021) 800 07 40*
@ *sofitelrio@infolink.com-br*

From the terraces of this hotel, now undergoing refurbishment, there is an unrestricted view of the entire Copacabana beach ➡ 80, and a bird's-eye view of the interior of the fort (which can be visited). In addition to its functional rooms, the Sofitel offers two swimming pools, one to catch the sun in the morning, the other in the afternoon. The tearoom is a good place to stop and take some refreshment after sunbathing. The gourmet restaurant is run by Roland Villard, formerly of the Pré Catelan in Paris.

Hotel Debret (8)
Avenida Atlântica, 3564 / Alm. Gonçalves, 5 - Copacabana
☎ 522 01 32 ➡ 521 08 99

80 rooms ● *15 suites R$ 87,50* 🔲 🔲 🔲 🔲 🔲 🔲 🔲 *Mucama* 🔲 *Terrace* 🔲
🔲 🔲 @ *fales@debret.com*

The colonial-style decoration of the Hotel Debret is a distant reminder of the French designer who was invited to Rio in 1816 as part of an "artistic mission" ➡ 76. The hotel offers rooms with a view of the beach at reasonable rates, but be sure to ask for a room on the seaward side.

Rio Atlântica (9)
Avenida Atlântica, 2964 - Copacabana ☎ 248 63 32 ➡ 255 64 10

108 rooms ●●●● *120 suites R$ 525* 🔲 🔲 🔲 🔲 🔲 🔲 🔲 🔲 🔲 🔲 🔲
🔲 🔲 @ *http://www.mhwnet.com.br/rioatlantica ; rioatlantica@net.gate.com.br*

This fine modern hotel is owned by Roberto Merinho, boss of the world's fourth largest communications group, Globo, some of whose programs are recorded here. The Rio Atlântico offers huge, comfortable rooms, in a setting geared to business needs. ★ The rooms overlooking the sea have balconies, which are an ideal place for breakfast. Enjoy the all-round view from the hotel roof terrace, where there is a large, inviting pool.

Not forgetting

■ **Rio Othon Palace Hotel (10)** Avenida Atlântica, 3264 - Copacabana ☎ 522 15 22 ➡ 522 16 97 ●●●● *Tourists and business people patronize this hotel, housed in a high-rise building overlooking Copacabana beach. Heated pool on the 30th floor. Craft items for sale on the calçadão (the beach-side sidewalk).* ■ **Windsor Palace (11)** Rua Domingos Ferreiras, 6 - Copacabana ☎ 548 00 98 ➡ 257 93 73 ●●● *Friendly, middle-of-the-range hotel, with a pool on the 17th floor.* ■ **Premier Copacabana Hotel (12)** Rua Tonelero, 205 - Copacabana ☎ 548 85 81 ➡ 547 41 39 ●● *A quiet hotel in a street lying parallel to the Avenida Atlântica, five minutes from the beach.* ■ **Olinda Othon (13)** Avenida Atlântica, 2230 - Copacabana ☎ ➡ 257 18 90 ●● *A pleasant hotel, and a fine-looking building.*

In the area

Ipanema is, of course, well known as the cradle of the bossa-nova. Nowadays it is a lively district with many businesses and restaurants. The sun rises on the Arpoador (Copacabana direction) and sets behind the mountain of the "two brothers" (Dois Irmãos), on whose slopes is the favela of Vidigal.

Where to stay

Cæsar Park (14)

Avenida Vieira Souto, 460 - Ipanema ☎ 525 25 25 ➡ 521 60 00

P *221 rooms* ●●●●● *32 suites R$ 600* 🅿 ⬛ 🅾 ⬛ 📷 �🏨 *on request*
🛏 Ⅲ 🍴 *Tiberius* 🅈 *Dionisios* ✕ ✚ 🏊 ⊞ 🎿 🅅 *0800 21 07 89*
@ *caesar.ipanema@openlink.com.br*

The Cæsar Park is now regarded as Rio's top luxury hotel. The service is of a very high standard. This is one of the few Ipanema hotels with a beach-side location. The Petronius restaurant ➡ 34, which has an unrestricted view of the beach, is well known for its feijoada. The hotel chosen by Madonna, the Rolling Stones and other big spenders.

Sol Ipanema (15)

Avenida Vieira Souto, 320 - Ipanema ☎ 523 00 95 ➡ 247 84 84

90 rooms ●●●●● *4 suites* ● *R$ 400* 🅿 ⬛ 🅾 ⬛ 📷 🏨 Ⅲ 🍴 *Evidence*
🅈 *Lobby Bar* ✕ ✚ 🏊 🅅 *0800 11 00 98* @ *hotel@solipanema.com.br*

The Sol Ipanema, which has recently become part of the Best Western group, may be the answer if you are looking for a middle-range hotel near to the beach. It offers decent service, though the setting is not outstanding. Opposite the hotel, lookout post 9 is a favorite meeting place of carioca youth, so you can be sure of local color.

Everest Rio (16)

Rua Prudente de Morais, 1117 - Ipanema ☎ 523 22 82 ➡ 521 31 98

P *R$ 11 per day. 156 rooms* ●●●●● *9 suites R$ 365* 🅿 ⬛ 🅾 ⬛ 📷
Ⅲ *on request* 🏨 Ⅲ 🍴 🅈 *Da Piscina, Lobby* ✚ 🏊 ⊞ 🎿 🅅 *0800 24 44 85*
@ *everest@marlim.com.br*

Tucked away on the first street running parallel to the beach, the Everest is relatively quiet. A modern, functional hotel, though not perhaps very exciting, it may suit the needs of the business traveler.

Country Residence Service (17)

Rua Prudente de Morais, 1700 - Ipanema ☎ 511 52 52 ➡ 259 09 43

P *23 apartments* ●●●● 🅿 ⬛ 🅾 ⬛ 📷 ✕ 🏊 ✕ 🎿

This luxury apartment hotel stands opposite the highly select Country Club. ★ The individual apartments are very well appointed, with views of the sea as a backdrop.

Not forgetting

■ **Monsieur Le Blond (18)** Avenida Bartolomeu Mitre, 455 - Leblon
☎ 529 30 30 ➡ 529 32 20 ●● *Good quality apartment hotel. Reservations essential.* ■ **Praia Ipanema (19)** Avenida Vieira Souto, 706 - Ipanema
☎ 239 68 89 105 rooms ●●●● *All rooms have sea views. Well situated, with excellent security arrangements.* ■ **Arpoador Inn (20)** Rua Francisco Otaviano, 177 - Ipanema ☎ 523 00 60 ➡ 511 50 94 ● *The Arpoador Inn has two distinct advantages: it is right on the sea front, and room prices are reasonable. Good view of the Arpoador headland, a favorite spot of surfers.*

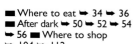

■ Where to eat ➡ 34 ➡ 36
■ After dark ➡ 50 ➡ 52 ➡ 54
➡ 56 ■ Where to shop
➡ 104 ➡ 112

14

14

20

In the area
Of the city center's former grand hotels, only the Glória now survives. Though very busy during the day, the center is virtually empty after office hours.
■ Where to eat ➡ 42 ➡ 44 ➡ 46 ■ After dark ➡ 52 ➡ 54 ➡ 56
■ What to see ➡ 66 ➡ 68 ➡ 70 ➡ 72 ➡ 78 ➡ 50

Where to stay

Hotel Glória (21)
Rua do Russel, 632 - Glória ☎ 555 72 72 ➡ 555 72 82

🅿 650 rooms ●●●● 19 suites R$ 430 🔲🔲🔲🔲🔲🔲🔲🔲🔲🔲 Colonial 🔲
🔲 🔲 🔲 🔲 🔲 🔲 🔲 @ hgloria@iis.com.br

One of the town's oldest establishments, the Glória lost its sea-front position in the 1920s, when work was begun to reclaim the surrounding area. It nevertheless retains the old-fashioned charm of a shore hotel. One of its two swimming pools has a grandstand view over the gardens of Flamengo park ➡ 72, designed by Burle Marx, and the Glória marina. The other pool, between the annexe and the hotel proper, has an agreeable tropical bar. The splendid Colonial restaurant is designed on the lines of a 17th-century Brazilian residence. ★ Ask for a room in the older part of the hotel, which is more distinguished and spacious.

Novo Mundo (22)
Praia do Flamengo, 20 - Flamengo ☎ 557 62 26 ➡ 265 23 69

🔲 Catete 🅿 6 R$/day. 230 rooms ●● 15 suites R$ 136 🔲🔲🔲🔲🔲🔲🔲
🔲🔲 Flamboyant 🔲 Grand Prix 🔲🔲🔲 @ reservas@hotelnovomundo-rio.com.br

The Novo Mundo is not far from the Museu de República ➡ 74, the former presidential palace. For almost fifty years, it has been a haunt of Brazilian politicians. ★ The most desirable rooms are at the side of the hotel, overlooking the Catete park, with the bay in the background.

Flórida (23)
Rua Ferreira Viana, 81 - Flamengo ☎ 556 52 42 ➡ 285 57 77

🔲 Catete 🅿 224 rooms ● 8 suites R$ 105 🔲🔲🔲🔲🔲🔲🔲 Babouska
🔲🔲🔲🔲

The permanently busy district of Catete, near the Largo do Machado, is authentically Brazilian in flavor. Renovated in 1991, the Flórida is a tasteful modern hotel, charging reasonable prices. The Museu da República ➡ 74 is nearby. The hotel has a pleasant terrace and swimming pool.

Guanabara Palace Hotel (24)
Avenida Presidente Vargas, 392 - Centro ☎ 518 03 33 ➡ 516 15 82

🔲 Uruguaiana ; Presidente Vargas 🅿 301 rooms ●● 3 suites R$ 185 🔲 free for residents 🔲🔲🔲🔲🔲🔲🔲 Malaga 🔲🔲🔲🔲🔲

In the center of the business district, near the church of the Candelária ➡ 78, the Guanabara has recovered some of its prestige after a recent refurbishment. This area is particularly deserted at night and on weekends.

Not forgetting

■ **Hotel Santa Tereza (25)** Rua Almirante Alexandrino, 660 - Santa Tereza ☎ 508 90 88 ● *In the Santa Tereza district. A rare boarding house surviving from the end of last century. Though showing its age, it is well worth visiting for its view of the town and unique environment. Difficult to get to though.*
■ **Aeroporto Othon (26)** Avenida Beira Mar, 280 - Castelo ☎ 210 32 53 ●●● *Handy for travelers needing a hotel close to Santos Dumont airport ➡ 8.*

■ Where
to shop
➡ 1110
➡ 1112

Above: view of
Flamengo park
from the Novo
Mundo hotel.
Left: lobby of
the Hotel
Santa Tereza.

In the area

The coastline around Rio is very varied. To the southwest is the Costa Verde (Paraty, Angra dos Reis and Ilha Grande, the largest island in the bay of Angra). To the northeast are the vast beaches of the Costa do Sol and the Búzios peninsula. ■ Further afield ➡ 92 ➡ 94

➡ Where to stay

33

30

35

Pousada Pardieiro (27)

Rua do Comércio, 74 - Paraty
☎ (024) 371 13 70
📠 (024) 371 11 39
25 rooms
●● 🖃
Inn tucked away in an old colonial residence. The rooms are laid out around patios and well furnished in the Portuguese style. There is a pool in the garden.

Pousada d`o Príncipe (27)

Avenida Roberto Silveira, 289 - Paraty

☎ (024) 371 22 66
📠 (024) 371 21 20
34 rooms ● 🖃
Just 250 yards from the historic town center, this property belonging to prince Dom João Orléans e Bragance conceals a comfortable, elegant, interior behind an unprepossessing façade.

Hotel Fazenda Paraíso do Sol (29)

Praia Saco das Palmas - Ilha Grande
☎ (021) 262 12 26

➡ (021) 220 67 04
32 chalets ●●
(transportation and full board) 🖃
In an enchanting seaside location A steep, narrow path leads to the famous Lopes Mendes beach, a mecca for surfers and nature lovers. Rooms must be booked in advance.

Club Med Rio das Pedras (30)

Rodovia BR 101 Rio-Santos (c. 30 miles out of Rio) - Manguaratiba
☎ (021) 688 50 50
🔽 0800 21 37 82

➡ (021) 688 33 33
324 rooms ●●●
(R$1169 per week)
🖃 @ clubmed@ caixapostal.com.br
Book through normal Club Med channels. The village is reserved for those who have booked their vacation in advance. This establishment is well up to standard. It has a rock-fringed private beach, and the colorful little buildings are set in a delightful garden.

Portobello (31)

Rodovia BR 101

33

28

34

Rio-Santos (30 miles out of Rio)
☎ (021) 689 30 00
85 rooms ●●●
▣ ✽
A luxury hotel built around a huge old house, which also serves as lobby and restaurant.
It overlooks a magnificent sandy beach.

Pousada Mestre Augusto (32)

Estrada do Contorno, 4509 - Búzios
☎ (024) 365 06 19
➠ (024) 365 28 36
6 rooms
●●● ▣ ✽
A charming little seaside inn, simple

and comfortable, with a homely feel to it. Reclining chairs overlooking the Atlantic Ocean invite you to take it easy. Breakfast, but no restaurant.

Galápagos Inn (33)

Praia João Fernandinho - Búzios
☎ (024) 623 61 61
➠ (024) 623 22 97
32 rooms ●●●●●
▣
The Galápagos is ideally situated, not a stone's throw from the Canto beach and the famous Rua das Pedras. Well appointed,

the hotel has 2 conference rooms, 2 saunas and a gym.

Pousada Quinta-Feira (34)

Rua Maria Joaquina, 405 - Búzios
☎ (024) 623 20 68
➠ (024) 623 26 07
10 rooms ● ▣ ✽
(no guests under 14 years old)
Set back from the Canto beach, 200 yards from the village. The rooms look out onto the garden and swimming pool.
★ The single suite has a terrace and sea view. No

restaurant, but there is a coffee-shop and a bar.

Pousada Casas Brancas (35)

Morro do Humaitá, 10 - Búzios
☎ (024) 623 14 58
➠ (024) 623 21 47
30 rooms
●●● ▣ ✽
★ This pousada has one of the finest views of Búzios, and is not too expensive. The terrace is a bewitching spot. The village and small beach of Ossos are no distance.

In the area

A mountain road leads to Petrópolis, once the summer residence of the emperor Dom Pedro II. It is now a retreat for well-heeled cariocas, who go there to escape the heat. Farther north the road takes you into the Minas Gerais. Ouro Prêto and other historic towns were built in the

➡ Where to stay

39   39

Locanda della Mimosa (36)

Alameda das Mimosas, 30 - Vale Florido - Petrópolis (km 71,5 of the BR-040 main road)
☎ *(024) 242 54 05*
➡ *(024) 242 54 05*
6 rooms ●●●●●
🔲 *(no guests under 16 years old)*
Quiet hotel with Italian sophistication. Good restaurant. Try the pizza on a Sunday evening before returning to Rio. Also take a look at the cellar, under the swimming pool, which has space for 30,000 bottles.

Pousada das Araras (37)

Estrada Bernardo Coutinho, 4570 - Araras - Petrópolis
☎ ➡
(024) 225 1143
6 rooms ●●●
🔲
Mountain retreat offering a high standard of comfort.

Rosa dos Ventos (38)

Route RJ-Teresópolis,
c. 17 miles north of Rio.
☎ *(021) 742 88 33*
➡ *(021) 742 81 74*
When booking from Rio ☎ *532 11 97*
40 rooms
●●●● full board
(no guests under 16 years old)
The only Brazilian member of the 'Relais et Châteaux' network. Accommodation is in chalets set in an immense park.

Solar da Ponte (39)

Praça das Mercês - Tiradentes MG
☎ *(032) 355 12 55*
➡ *(032) 355 12 01*
12 rooms ●●
🔲 *(no guests under 12 years old)*
Housed in an old planter's residence, this hotel has a distinctly English flavor, despite the setting. An excellent afternoon tea is served. Splendid garden with swimming pool.

Pousada Richard Rothe (40)

Rua Padre Toledo - Tiradentes MG
☎ *(032) 355 13 33*
7 rooms ●● 🔲

gold-rush days of the 17th and 18th centuries.

■ Further afield ➡ 92 ➡ 94

36

36

(no guests under 12 years old) Former colonial mansion, painstakingly restored, just a short walk from the Matriz. Situated in a quiet street with irregular paving stones. ★ Try the excellent *mineiro* breakfast with fromage frais and tropical fruits.

Pousada do Mondego (41)

Largo de Coimbra, 38 - Ouro Prêto MG

☎ (031) 551 20 40
➡ (031) 551 30 94
24 rooms ●● ▤
Opposite the church of São Francisco de Assis, near Tiradentes square, in the heart of Ouro Prêto, the hotel occupies a fine old mansion with comfortable rooms looking down over the valley. There is a craft market on the first floor. Pleasant but a bit on the expensive side.

Luxor Pousada (42)

Rua Dr Alfredo Baeta, 10 - Ouro Prêto MG
☎ ➡
(031) 551 22 44
16 rooms ● ▤
Below the town, near the Igreja de Conceição, is a charming hotel housed in an old mansion. The rooms are light and airy. ★ The restaurant is highly recommended. Be prepared for a strenuous walk, as the main monuments are in the upper town.

Pouso Chico Rey (43)

Rua Brig. Mosqueira, 90 - Ouro Prêto MG
☎ (031) 551 12 74
6 rooms ● ▤
This inn, opposite the Igreja Nossa Senhora do Carmo, and a short walk from one of Latin America's oldest theaters, is owned by a Dane. It still has the décor and furnishings of a local dignitary's house. Pleasant breakfast room. The stairs are rather steep!

Opening hours

Generally speaking, restaurants are open non-stop from noon until late in the evening. No one will bat an eyelid if you drop in for lunch at 4pm!

➡ Where to eat

Tipping

A service charge (10%) is generally included in the bill. If you need a receipt, ask for a *nota fiscal.*

"Comida a quilo"

(Meals by the kilo) ➡ 36
Pay by weight! This is the custom in many restaurants (especially in the business districts).

"Pão de queijo"

Not to be missed. Cheese rolls of this kind are made by all the local padarias (bakers). They can also be bought at a *casa do pão de queijo*, easily recognized by its sign. Try one *simples* (plain), *recheado* (with filling), or *bem quentinho* (straight from the oven).

49
Restaurants

THE INSIDER'S FAVORITES

"Couvert"

This is the expression used for the various *petiscos* (tidbits) served before you place your order. Take note! This *couvert opcional* is served as a matter of course and costs around R$ 4 per person. If you do not want it, tell the waiter.

INDEX BY SPECIALTY

- less than R$ 15
- ● ● R$ 16–R$ 25
- ● ● ● R$ 26–R$ 35
- ● ● ● ● R$ 36–R$ 45
- ● ● ● ● ● more than R$ 45

Brazilians enjoy a good filling meal, and some dishes may seem rather heavy. Brazilian cooking comes in different shapes and sizes, depending on region (Amazonia, Nordeste, Minas Gerais, Santa Caterina) and historical influence. However, there is no typically carioca cuisine. In Rio, you will find a mixture of different Brazilian styles and what is referred to as *cozinha*

➡ Where to eat

The national dish

Feijão com arroz e faroza (white rice with black beans and smoked bacon, well sprinkled with cassava flour) is the basis of Brazilian cookery. This dish, accompanied by *frango* (chicken), *carne* (steak) or *peixe* (fish, usually fried), is served at any hour of day or night, every day of the week.
Feijoada, once a meal for slaves, made with the offcuts of pork, has become the national dish, and is traditionally served on Saturday. Often compared with French cassoulet, it tends to be rather heavy. It consists of an assortment of items deriving from pig and cow: dried salted beef, sausage, smoked pork chops, tongue, ox-tail, pigs' ears and trotters, together with *arroz* and *feijão*, green cabbage cut into strips, rounds of orange and fried cassava, all sprinkled with *farofa*. The meal begins with a small glass of *caldo do feijão* (the juice in which the beans were cooked), which is drunk scalding hot. People then serve themselves from the large terra cotta pots. Purists sprinkle their *feijoada* with marinated chili peppers (*pimenta malagueta*), but those with more delicate palates will stick at a few token drops.

Regional cooking

The robust **comida miniera** (the cuisine of the Minas Gerais region) tends to be rather spicy. Its mainstay is pork (*leitão*, sucking pig), with vegetables such as *couve* (a green cabbage with large flat leaves). For those who like their steaks rare, a specialty of Rio Grande do Sul is **churrasco** (listed as **rodizio** in restaurants where you can eat as much as you like) – lightly barbecued beef seasoned with sea salt. Any *churrasco* worthy of the name is served with smoked sausage and chicken or pork, and *molho à campanha* (onions and tomatoes marinated in vinegar).

internacional – not a very helpful term!

African influence

Palm oil (*azeite de dendê*, rather heavy on the stomach), coconut milk and chili peppers are key ingredients in many dishes: *moqueca*, from the Bahia region, is made with shrimp (prawns) or crab simmered in a thick tomato and onion sauce, and flavored with palm oil and coconut milk; *vatapá* consists of fish and shrimp (prawns) cooked in palm oil and coconut milk, with green vegetables such as *quiabo* (gombo). For those with a sweet tooth, *quindim* is a bright yellow coconut tart with a crisp base.

Portuguese influence

From their Portuguese colonizers, the Brazilians have inherited a taste for *bacalhau* (cod), now reserved for special occasions because prices are prohibitive, and some very sugary desserts. *Cozido* (a kind of stew) is served with *batata doce* (sweet potato), *abóbora* (pumpkin), *bananas da terra*, *chuchu* (chayote, a member of the squash family), and sometimes *couve flor* (cauliflower).

Fruits

Fruit is an important part of the Brazilian diet, eaten at breakfast (*café de manhã*), as a dessert or in the form of fruit juice (*suco*). Nordeste province has many unusual fruits (*cupuaçu*, *pitanga*...), which are not easily obtained in Rio. However, tourists will find an abundance of the more common tropical fruits, such as *manga* (mango), *mamão* (papaw), *abacaxi* (pineapple, not to be confused with *abacate*, avocado, which is served for dessert as a sugary cream or in ice-cream), *melão* (melon), *caju* (they extract the juice and use the nut), or the common-or-garden *banana*, especially delicious in this part of the world.

Parallel with Ipanema's main shopping street, the Rua Visconde de Pirajá, runs the much quieter, more residential Rua Barão da Torre, where many of the best restaurants are concentrated. On weekends, they open at 2pm. ▣ Where to stay ➡ 20 ➡ 22 ▣ After dark ➡ 50 ➡ 52 ➡ 54

➡ Where to eat

Satyricon (1)

Rua Barão da Torre, 192
☎ 521 09 55
Fish, seafood
●●●●● ▣
🕐 Mon. 7pm–2am; Tue.–Sun. noon–2am.
For the last fifteen years, the Satyricon has specialized in freshly caught fish. Italian and Japanese food is also on the menu.

Porcão (2)

Rua Barão da Torre, 278
☎ 522 09 99
Rodizio ●●● ▣
🕐 Daily 11.30am –last customer
An army of waiters serve meat of all kinds impaled on long spits: *picanha*, filet mignon with cheese, *miminha*, *chuleta* with garlic, pork loin, chicken legs, etc. Take your pick.

Mme Butterfly (3)

Rua Barão da Torre, 472
☎ 267 43 47
Fish, seafood
●●● ▣
🕐 Daily noon–2am
A classic Japanese restaurant. Dishes include *sashimi*, *tepanhyaky* and, of course, sushi – traditional or served in highly imaginative style. Try the *temp roll*: hot sushi stuffed with shrimp *tempura*, or – even more way out – sushi fried in breadcrumbs.

Casa da Feijoada (4)

Rua Prudente de Moraes, 10
☎ 523 49 94
Feijoada
●● ▣
🕐 Daily noon–2am
Feijoada is traditionally served on Saturdays.
★ Here you can try it any day of the week in the typical setting of a tiny restaurant located just a short walk from the beach.
It is served in earthenware pots with all the trimmings and laced with lemon or passion-fruit *batida*.

Le Panetier (5)

Rua Vinícius de Moraes, 121
☎ 521 08 24
Bistrot ● ▣
🕐 Mon.–Sat. 8am–8pm; Sun. 9am–6pm
Ideal for a quick lunch in a semi-bistro, semi-tearoom setting. Sandwiches, salads, quiches, pastries and ice-creams are made and served in traditional French style.

Gula-Gula (6)

Rua Aníbal de Mendonça, 132
☎ 259 30 84
Bistro ● ▣
🕐 Mon. noon–4pm Sun., Tue.–Thu. noon–midnight; Fri.–Sat. noon–1am
The restaurant is packed at lunchtime on account of its salads and quiches. ★ Try the highly popular 'meia-meia' (half and half), two kinds of salad on one plate.

Marius Ipanema (7)

Rua Francisco Otaviano, 96
☎ 521 05 00
Rodizio ●●● ▣
🕐 Daily 11.45am–1am
Churrasco served in a sophisticated atmosphere. The *rodizio*-style meats are presented on plates, not on spits.

■ What to see ➡ 80 ■ Where to shop ➡ 104 ➡ 112

Grottamare (8)

Rua Gomes Carneiro, 132
☎ 522 31 86
Fish, seafood
●●● ▣
◐ Mon.–Fri.
7pm–0.30am;
Sat., Sun., and
public holidays
noon–0.30am
One of Rio's
best seafood
restaurants if
you want plenty
to eat without
formality.
Labyrinth of
rooms with
rustic décor.

Caffé Felice (9)

Rua Gomes
Carneiro, 30
☎ 522 77 49
Italian cuisine
●● ▣ Ⓨ
◐ Tue.–Thu.,
Sun. 10am–1am;
Fri.–Sat. 10am–last
customer
Designer décor
beach house
which has

somehow
managed to
survive the threat
of property
speculation.
A favorite with
the young, trendy
crowd from the
"Zona Sul".

Pulcinella (10)

Rua Farme de
Amoedo, 102
☎ 523 37 92
Italian cuisine
●●●● ▣
◐ Tues.–Sat.
7pm–2am;
Sun., public
holidays noon–2am
In this rustic
cantina with
wood-and-plaster
décor chef
Luciano Pollarini
feasts his regular
customers on
pasta and risotto
dishes. Tables can
be booked on
weekdays until
7pm.

In the area

Leblon may be an extension of Ipanema, but the atmosphere is subtly different, with fewer fashionable boutiques and more small shops meeting everyday needs. ■ Where to stay ➡ 22 ■ After dark ➡ 50 ➡ 52 ■ What to see ➡ 80 ■ Where to shop ➡ 104 ➡ 112

Where to eat

Garcia & Rodrigues (11)
Avenida Ataulfo de Paiva, 1251 - Leblon ☎ 512 81 88

French cuisine ●●● ▢ 🕐 *Daily 9am–midnight*

It would be hard to find better value anywhere in Rio. The French chef Christophe Lidy excels in fish cookery. For proof of his skills, just try his lightly cooked tuna mignonette. And the homemade rolls served throughout the meal are little short of perfection (Christophe is also a master baker). The red and yellow décor of the room is reminiscent of New York or London. The tables at the entrance tempt the passer-by to stop for a quick snack or try the take-out specialties, before buying a few bottles of wine on the mezzanine floor. Slimmed-down menu at lunch time; reservations essential in the evening.

Antiquarius (12)
Rua Aristides Espínola, 19 - Leblon ☎ 294 10 49 ➡ 512 57 56

Portuguese cuisine ●●●●● ▢ 🕐 *Daily noon–2am* ▯

This sophisticated establishment, graced with fine furniture and curios, attracts the cream of carioca society, from the world of business to the entertainment industry. They come to savor its Portuguese delicacies, among which cod features prominently. The bar offers some delicious snacks, including *bolinhos de bacalhau* (cod croquettes) and *patinhas de caranguejo* (crab pincers in bread crumbs). ★ The Antiquarius is also an antiques dealer, so do not be surprised if you leave with one of the display items under your arm.

Alvaro's Bar (13)
Avenida Ataulfo de Paiva, 500 - Leblon ☎ 294 21 48

Bistro ● ▢ 🕐 *Daily 11am–2am*

A prime example of the traditional carioca bistro, the great thing about Alvaro's is not so much the décor as the famous *pastéis* served there (fried turnovers stuffed with meat, cheese or shrimp, costing R$ 1 a piece). Eat them piping hot, with your fingers and plenty of paper napkins!

Celeiro (14)
Rua Dias Ferreira, 199 - Leblon ☎ 274 78 43

Bistro ● ▢ 🕐 *Daily Mon.– Tues. 11am–10.30pm; Wed.–Sat. 11am–6pm*

This establishment's proud boast is that it uses only the finest ingredients in its fragrant salads: chicken with cumin, zucchini with garlic, fried vegetables with balsamic vinegar. Some of the tables have been moved out onto the terrace, making more room in the main restaurant, whose light-wood furnishings create the atmosphere of an Austrian chalet. The Celeiro is a *comida a quilo* – you pay for your food by weight!

Not forgetting

■ **Jobi (15)** Avenida Ataulfo de Paiva, 1166 - Leblon ☎ 274 05 47 ●●● *This bistro, with its terrace on Leblon's main shopping street, has been in business for forty years.*

36

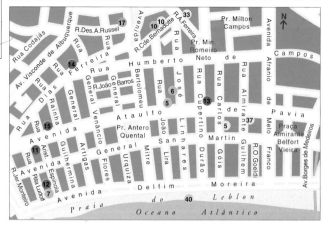

In the area

While the Ipanema side of the Lago, with its row of café terraces, has all the atmosphere of the beach, the Jardim Botânico side, at the foot of the mountain, is more countrified. ■ After dark ➡ 52 ➡ 54 ➡ 56
■ What to see ➡ 82 ➡ 86 ■ Where to shop ➡ 102 ➡ 106 ➡ 112

Where to eat

Bar Lagoa (16)
Avenida Epitácio Pessoa, 1674 - Lagoa ☎ 523 11 35

Bistro ● ▣ ▯ ⏱ *Daily noon-2am* ☘

Meeting place of carioca artists and intellectuals, the bar Lagoa is proud of its 63-year history, and its listed Art Deco interior. It all adds to the poetry of the place, which is famous for its *chope* (draught beer), reputed to be the best in Rio. Once you have appreciated the cariocas' enthusiasm for *chope estupidamente gelado* (excessively chilled), the success of this lakeside venue will be no surprise. The clientele tends to be young and fashionable. To feel at home, order a *salsichão com salada de batatas* (sausage, potato salad), and at least one *chope*.

Claude Troisgros (17)
Rua Custódio Serrão, 62 - Jardim Botânico ☎ 537 85 82

⚄ *French cuisine* ●●●●● ▣ ⏱ *Mon.–Fri. noon–3pm, 7.30pm–0.30am; Sat. 7.30pm–0.30am* ▮

The food Claude Troisgros serves in his little restaurant is a delight to the eyes as well as the palate. Ably seconded by Antonio Costa da Silva, he offers an inventive style of cookery, discreetly supplementing French gastronomy with products from the local Brazilian market: roast fillet of *cherne* with tomatoes, yam mousseline, vegetable marrow ravioli with almond butter, cheese cake with guava coulis. When Bill Clinton paid an official visit to Brazil, Claude was in his element. ★ A simplified version of the menu is available at lunchtime.

Photochart (18)
Jóquei Clube, Praça Santos Dumont, 31 - Gávea ☎ 512 22 47

International cuisine ●●● ▣ ⏱ *Daily noon until last customer leaves* ☘

Magnificently situated in Rio's hippodrome, the restaurant looks straight out onto the paddock, where you can watch the horses parade before a race. There are television screens to enable gamblers to follow the fortunes of their favorites without sacrificing the pleasures of the table. The cuisine is international, but with a distinctly Italian flavor. Some lighter dishes are also available.

Not forgetting

■ **Guimas (19)** Rua José Macedo Soares, 5 - Gávea ☎ 274 50 34 ●●●
A former dive now transformed into a bistro serving decent food in pleasant surroundings.
■ **Botequim (20)** Rua Visconde de Caravelas, 184 - Botafogo ☎ 286 33 91 ●● *Popular bistro with a relaxed atmosphere. Varied menu.*
■ **Amarcord (21)** Rua Maria Quitéria, 136 - Lagoa ☎ 287 03 35 ●●●●
Italian cuisine and an unrestricted view of the Lagoa. Artificial rain on the windows to keep the veranda cool.
■ **Allons Enfants (22)** Rua Visconde de Carandaí – Jardim Botânico ☎ 239 33 97 ●●● *Authentic Brittany-inspired French cuisine, with the addition of some dishes from southwest France (cassoulets and foie gras). Excellent value for money.*

Have fun doodling
on the tables at the
Guimas restaurant
(right)!

Having lost some of its prestige to Ipanema and Leblon, Copacabana is no longer quite such a fashionable place to eat. Its restaurants are either very traditional or very touristy. However, the Copacabana Palace and the Meridian hotel have two of the best chefs in town.

 # Where to eat

Marius Leme (23)
Avenida Atlântica, 290-B - Leme ☎ 542 23 93

Meat, rodizio ●●● ▤ ◷ *Daily 11.45am–1am* ▯

The 1970s aluminum décor of this *churrascaria* may be rather off-putting, but it is soon forgotten when the *rodizio* begins. You order your meat and side-dishes by writing your selection on a note-pad and giving it to the waiter at the start of the meal. There is a long list to choose from!

Le Saint-Honoré (24)
Hôtel Le Méridien, Avenida Atlântica, 1020 - Copacabana
☎ 275 99 22

▤ *French cuisine* ●●●●● ▤ ◷ *Mon.–Sat. 8pm–1am* ▯ ▯ ▨

The first thing that strikes you about the Saint-Honoré is its breathtaking view, with the whole length of Copacabana beach ➡ 80 lit up at your feet (the restaurant only opens in the evening). The spectacular backdrop and luxurious setting are well matched by the cooking of Pierre Landry, who is advised on the running of the restaurant by top chef Paul Bocuse. Among the delights on the menu, which changes with the seasons, are smoked salmon à la minute, crème froide au caviar, scallops in parsley sauce, and pigeon with cabbage and foie gras. ★ The restaurant puts on a different fixed-price menu every week. Be sure to book in advance for a table near the window.

Cipriani (25)
Copacabana Palace, Avenida Atlântica, 1702 ☎ 548 70 70

▤ *Italian cuisine* ●●●●● ▤ ◷ *Daily 12.30–2.30pm; 8pm–midnight* ▯ ▣

The chef at the Cipriani, Francesco Carli, introduces his guests to the very best of northern Italian cooking: eggplant and goat-cheese tart with a coulis of tomatoes, black tagliatelle with seafood, filet of salmon with onion sauce, risotto with squid and, of course, *tiramisú*, light and frothy in its chocolate nest. The palatial atmosphere of this top restaurant is enhanced by paintings of Rio in colonial times, the magnificent high-ceilinged room with its chandeliers, the piano playing quietly in the background, and the view of the swimming-pool.

Not forgetting

■ **La Pomme d'or (26)** Rua Sá Ferreira, 22 - Copacabana ☎ 522 05 48 ●●● *Brazilian architect Oscar Niemeyer is a regular. His favorite is Rabada (oxtail stew).* ■ **Da Brambini (27)** Avenida Atlântica, 514 - Leme ☎ 275 43 46 ●●● *Small Italian bistro overlooking the beach. Tends to attract a well-heeled clientele at lunchtime.* ■ **Pérgula (28)** Copacabana Palace, Avenida Atlântica, 1702 - Copacabana ☎ 585 87 44 ●●●●● *Delightful setting for an unpretentious lunch on the pool-side terrace. Well-stocked seafood buffet.* ■ **Montecarlo (29)** Rua Duvivier, 21 - Copacabana ☎ 541 41 47 ●●●● *A favorite with carioca intellectuals, who come here to enjoy feijoada on Saturdays (never before 4pm).* ■ **La Trattoria (30)** Rua Fernando Mendes, 7-A - Copacabana ☎ 255 33 19 ●● *Green and white chequered tablecloths. Italian food at reasonable prices.*

- Where to stay ➡ 18 ➡ 20
- What to see ➡ 50 ➡ 52

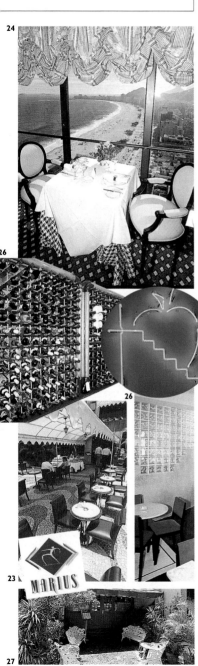

In the area

Designed by landscape architect Burie-Marx, the Aterro do Flamengo, a narrow strip of land won from the sea which links the Centro to the Zona Sul, is more than just an expressway. It is a "botanical Noah's ark", with exotic trees and shrubs skillfully arranged to form a spectacular setting.

Where to eat

Kotobuki (31)
Avenida Pasteur, 86 - Botafogo ☎ 541 00 01

Japanese cuisine ●● ▣ ◑ *Mon.–Fri. noon–4.30pm, 7pm–1am; Sat.–Sun. 1pm–midnight*

This four-storey restaurant is simple and unadorned, but the lack of decoration is more than made up for by the view from the terrace of Botafogo bay, and the quality of the food. ★ The fare on offer depends on the time of day: *almoço executivo* (business lunch), all the sushi *rodizio* and *sashimi* you can eat in the evenings, happy hour with 30% reductions from 7pm to 9pm. In the evening, the roof terrace (a good climb) is always crowded. Dining areas can be reserved. This chain runs several restaurants in Rio.

Mercado São José (32)
Rua das Laranjeiras, 90 - Flamengo ☎ 558 28 68

Bistro ● ▣ ◑ *Tue.–Sun. 11am–midnight*

Charming local market, with a number of small restaurants set out around a patio. Seated outside under awnings, you can enjoy grilled squid or an excellent pizza, washed down with a *chope* of chilled beer.

Yorubá (33)
Rua Arnaldo Quintela, 94 - Botafogo ☎ 295 51 93

Brazilian cuisine (Bahia) ●●●●● ▣ ◑ *Wed.–Fri. 1noon–3pm, 7pm–1am; Sat. noon–5pm, 7pm–1am; Sun. noon–8pm*

In a picturesque setting of African-style sculptures and papier mâché masks, colorful cook Neide Santos serves the best of Afro-Bahain cuisine: *moqueca de siri* (crab fricassee), fish in coconum, *piri-piri* (rice and fried shrimp), *cocada preta* (coconut dessert). An appetizing fragrance wafts out into the street!

Aprazível (34)
Rua Aprazível, 62 Santa Tereza ☎ ➡ 508 91 74

International cuisine ●●● ▣ ◑ *Wed.–Fri. 8pm–midnight, Sat.–Sun. 1pm–midnight*

Tucked away in Santa Tereza, with its narrow backstreets and sloping gardens is this enchanting restaurant in a luxuriant natural setting with 100-year old trees. The menu is simple but carefully chosen. There is the added bonus of *chorinho* concerts ➡ 49 on Thursday evenings.

Not forgetting

■ **Alcaparra (35)** Praia do Flamengo, 150 - Flamengo ☎ 558 39 37 ●●●● *The best known of the Flamengo's restaurants, frequented by politicians and businesspeople.* ■ **Círculo Militar da Praia Vermelha (36)** Praça General Tiburcio, s/n - Urca ☎ 295 33 97 ● *One of the most outstanding views in Rio: Sugar Loaf ➡ 84, the ocean and islands. You would never think there were eleven million people so close behind you.*

- Where to stay ➡ 24
- After dark ➡ 54 ■ What to see ➡ 72 ➡ 74 ➡ 84 ➡ 86
- Where to shop ➡ 102 ➡ 112

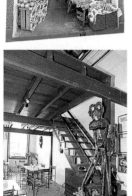

The Circulo Militar (left) is one of the best places for a view of the Sugar Loaf.

Be warned: restaurants in the Centro district have adapted their schedules to the needs of a primarily business clientele. They are open only on weekdays, at lunchtime. In compensation, several have instituted a happy hour. ■ After dark ➡ 52 ■ What to see ➡ 66 ➡ 70 ➡ 72

Where to eat

Alba Mar (37)
Praça Marechal Âncora, 184-186 ☎ 240 84 28

🐟 *Fish, seafood* ●●● ☐ 🕐 *Mon. 11.30am–4pm; Tue.–Sat. 11.30am–10pm* 🏊

The Alba Mar is a vestige of Rio's old municipal market, erected in the early years of the century in the Baltard style. Bought out in 1964 by a group of employees, the restaurant faithfully continues a long tradition of serving politicians, businessmen, and now tourists, who come to enjoy its fish and seafood specialties. ★ Through the narrow windows, there are magnificent views of the Ilha Fiscal and the Niterói bridge ➡ 84, and of ferries plying back and forth. Many of those who took over the restaurant in the 1960s are still shareholders today, including the chef and the maître d'hôtel. The restaurant is now a listed building.

Atrium (38)
Rua 19 de Fevereiro, 94 ☎ 286 21 06 ➡ 531 15 70

Ⓜ *Carioca* **International cuisine** ●● ☐ 🕐 *Mon.–Fri. 11.30am–3pm*

The Atrium occupies a vaulted room in the Paço Imperial museum ➡ 66, once the Portuguese viceroy's palace. As soon as you enter the quiet paved courtyard, the bustle of the business district is left behind. There are some succulent but not-too-heavy dishes on the menu: *farfale* with vegetables, *Berry filet* (filet of beef, berry fruits and palm-heart pancakes), fresh salmon *feuilleté*, and cheesecake with fruit coulis.

Geraes (39)
Rua do Ouvidor, 26 ☎ 242 86 10

Brazilian cuisine (Minas Gerais) ●●● ☐ 🕐 *Mon.–Fri. 11.30am–4pm*
Happy hour Wed.–Fri. 6.30–11pm **Buffet mineiro** *Wed., Thu., Fri.* 🍷

Despite its modern décor, the Geraes has retained some of the features of a former *sobrado*. Even if you speak only a little Portuguese, the voluble, ever-smiling chef, Mariza Horta, will gladly launch into a detailed description of the traditional *mineira* dishes, copious and beautifully prepared (portions are sufficient for two!): *galinha ao molho pardo* (jugged chicken), *feijão tropeiro* (garlic, onion, shallotts, cabbage, cubes of bacon, cassava flour and scrambled eggs), *vaca atolada* (rib of beef cooked in a thick sauce of tomatoes, garlic and onion), and, of course, all the traditional *mineiro* sweetmeats.

Not forgetting

■ **Cabaça Grande (40)** Rua do Ouvidor, 12 ☎ 231 23 01 ●●●●
Some fine fish and seafood specialties, if you can stand the neon strip-lighting.
■ **Churrascaria Sertão Gaucho (41)** Rua da Quitânda,
49-A ☎ 242 17 55 ●● *A traditional haunt of Rio's business community. Quality ingredients and generous portions.* ■ **Mercato (42)** Edifício da Bolsa de Valores, Praça XV de Novembro, 20 ☎ 414 11 60 ●●● *International cuisine with an Italian bias. Spectaclar view.* ■ **Champs Élysées (43)** Maison de France, Avenida Presidente Antônio Carlos, 58 (12th floor) ☎ 220 47 13 ●●● *This restaurant, run by two brothers from Gascony (Alain and Dominique Raymond), has an atmosphere typical of provincial France. Business clientele, good view.*

■ Where to shop ➧ 110
➧ 112

38

Atrium restaurante

39

37

37

38

43

Map labels:

R. do Rosário
R. do Ouvidor
R. da Quitanda
R. da Assembléia
Rua R Silva
Rua 7 de Setembro
Rua 1. de Março
R. do Carmo
R. Mercado
Avenida Presidente
Baía de Guanabara
Pr. XV
Av. Erasmo Braga
R. Mise ricordia
Praça Marechal Âncora
Kubitschek
Canoca
Avenida Nilo Peçanha
Praça do Expedicionário
Pr. Rui Barbosa
Pr. João Paulo II
Av. Almirante Barroso
Rua Marechal Aguinaldo
R. Pres. Antônio Carlos
Avenida México
Graça Aranha
Rua Debret
Rua Araújo Porto Alegre
Rua de Santa Luzia
Rua P. Lessa
Av. Churchill

24 3 39 40 1 38 42 34 2 41 9 25 11 13 16 43 37

In the area

The west side of the Rue 1ero de Março, typified by the bustle of the
Avenida Rio Branco, is in marked contrast with the calm of the Praça XV,
where the old colonial buildings house libraries and cultural centers.
■ Where to stay ➜ 24 ■ After dark ➜ 52 ➜ 54 ➜ 56 ■ What to see

 # Where to eat

Confeitaria Colombo (44)
Rua Gonçalves Dias, 32 - Centro ☎ 232 23 00

M *Carioca* **International cuisine** ●●● ▣ 🕑 *Mon.–Fri. 8am–7pm* 🎵

Founded in 1894, the Confeitaria Colombo was refurbished in 1913 in a
neo-French style using jacaranda wood. Not to be missed, it is one of the
most amazing places in South America. You arrive on foot (the area is
pedestrianized) to have lunch in the main dining room (serve yourself at
the buffet or choose from the menu) or, if you prefer a snack, for a
coxinha (fried chicken croquette) and a pastry, eaten standing at the
entrance. Tea is also served. For several generations, the Confeitaria
Colombo has been the smartest rendezvous in town.

Giuseppe (45)
Rua VII de Setembro, 65 - Centro ☎ 509 72 15

M *Carioca* **Italian cuisine** ●●● ▣ 🕑 *Mon.–Fri. noon–4pm* 🍸

In stark contrast with the busy ferment of Rio's business district, the
décor at Giuseppe's transports you to the heart of Rome: ocher walls,
bare stone, winter garden and a bubbling fountain. Not surprisingly, Italian
specialties feature prominently on the menu (carpaccio, gnocchi and
various pasta dishes). The Monday special is deliberately light – an
antidote to the excesses of the weekend! ★ The restaurant entrance is
set out in bistro style, offering sandwiches and salads and, on weekdays
from 4pm to 10pm, happy hour pizzas. It is best to book, but this is
possible only for the period between noon and 1pm.

Café do Teatro-Salão Assírio (46)
Praça Floriano s/n Centro ☎ 262 41 64

M *Cinelândia* **International cuisine** ●● ▣ 🕑 *Mon.–Fri. 11.30am–4pm*

Have you ever dreamed of being transported to Persepolis, to the
palace of Darius I, who ruled over the Persian empire in the 6th and
5th centuries BC? Then you must visit the Café du Théâtre Municipal,
where the décor, imported from France in 1906, is inspired by its
oriental pomp. Of particular interest are the extravagant greco-oriental
wall lamps and the alabaster globe pendants. However, the food is not in
keeping with the surroundings. *Feijoada* is served every Friday lunchtime.

Not forgetting

■ **Penafiel (47)** Rua Senhor dos Passos, 121 - Saara ☎ 224 68 70 ●●
*Founded in 1912, this establishment offers good-value Portuguese specialties, simply
served.*
■ **Senta aí (48)** Rua Barão de São Felix, 75 - Centro ☎ 233 83 58 ●●
*In Portuguese, 'Senta aí!' means 'Sit down there!'. The name gives the flavor of this
Portuguese restaurant, situated behind the main railway station, which serves a
sophisticated clientele in unpretentious surroundings.*
■ **Aspargus (49)** Clube dos Seguradores e Banqueiros, Rua Senador
Dantas, 74 - Centro ☎ 220 95 97 ●●●● *International cuisine. Housed on the
17th floor, the Asparagus offers an unrivaled view of the Christ ➜ 84 and the
Arcos da Lapa ➜ 76. The menu is very similar to that of the the Alcaparra ➜ 42.*

➤ 68 ➤ 70 ➤
72 ➤ 76 ➤ 78
■ Where to
shop ➤ 110
➤ 112

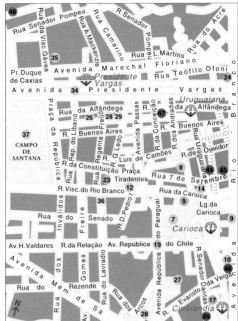

The Confeitaria Colombo
has Belgian and Venetian
fittings. The Assirio's are
from Paris.

Spring festivals

Information from Riotur ➡ 12
Free Jazz Rio A week of international jazz
Rio Cena Contemporanea Theater festival
Festival de Rio Film festival
Panorama Rio Arte de Dança Dance festival

➡ # After dark

Ticketronics reservations service

Call to reserve seats for the Caneção ➡ 54, the Teatro
Municipal ➡ 70, the Centro Cultural Banco do Brasil
➡ 70 and the Metropolitan ➡ 54.

Reservations ☎ 0800 78 16 16 🕐 *Mon.–Fri. 8am–5pm*
Tickets to be picked up at Shell gas stations equipped with
a *loja select* machine. Commission 15% of ticket price.

Gas stations

Posto Iate - Rua Reporter Nestor Moreira, 41 - Botafogo
Posto Hípica - Rua Jardim Botânico, 568 - Jardim Botânico
Posto Excede - Av. Epitácio Pessoa, 4630 - Lagoa
Posto Canário - Av. Afonso de Taunay, 801 - Barra da Tijuca

Information about shows and events in...
Revista Programa (Friday edition of the daily newspaper *Jornal do Brasil*)
Rio Show (Friday version of the newspaper *O Globo*)
Veja Rio (sold at news-stands on Sundays)

39

Nights out

THE INSIDER'S FAVORITES

Brazilian music

MPB (*Música Popular Brasileira*) Includes almost all contemporary trends in Brazilian music, apart from rock. The most popular singers are Chico Buarque and Elis Regina.
Bossa-nova Born, according to Antonio Carlos (Tom) Jobim, of the encounter between the Brazilian samba and modern jazz. Tom Jobim and Vinícius de Moraes are the leading exponents.
Samba-canção or *samba de enredo*. Music with a syncopated dance rhythm. Cartola is undoubtedly the high priest.

Chorinho comes from the verb *chorar* (to weep), though the music — played by a group which includes *cavaquinho* (guitar), *pandeiro* (drum) and a wind instrument — is relatively light-hearted.
Pagode a form of popular singing derived from the original samba. Very much in fashion in recent years.
Tropicalistes In the 1970s, four singer/composers (Caetano Veloso, Gilberto Gil, Maria Bethania and Gal Costa) popularized this Bahian style of music.

Coconut milk, maté glacé and *chope* (beer) are the refreshments generally served from the kiosks along the *calçadão* (the broad sidewalk which follows the shore). Along the beach and in adjacent streets, the many bars of the Zona Sul come to life as soon as the sun goes down.

After dark

Lucas (1)

Avenida Atlântica, 3744 - Copacabana
☎ 521 47 05
🕐 Sun.–Thu. 11am–1am; Fri.–Sat. 11am–2am; closed Dec. 25

For three generations *cariocas* have been coming here in their beach wear. You can sit and watch life go by on the *calçadão* as you enjoy a generous portion of the famous *cozido* (a filling stew) and have a few beers.

Barril 1800 (2)

Avenida Vieira Souto, 110 - Ipanema
☎ 523 00 85
🕐 Daily 10am– last customer; Dec. 24 and 31 10am–5pm

Rated highly by both Cariocas and tourists. After a day at the beach, this is a good place to watch the sun go down behind the Dois Irmãos (two brothers), the two enormous rocky outcrops which dominate the beaches of Leblon and Ipanema ➡ 80.

Bofetada (3)

Rua Farme de Amoedo, 87-A - Ipanema
☎ 522 95 26 or 523 39 92
🕐 Daily 7am–4am

Portuguese *botequim* (small bar) in a busy Ipanema street. It attracts a mixed bag of regulars and *gringos* (tourists), who drink their beer standing outside on the sidewalk or at tables upstairs (air-conditioned)
★ A must for lovers of *chorinho* (a popular style of instrumental music), Monday evenings from 8pm to midnight.

Garota de Ipanema (4)

Rua de Vinícius de Moraes, 49 - Ipanema
☎ 523 37 87
🕐 Sun.–Thu. 11.30am–1am; Fri.- Sat. 11.30am– 1.30am

This is where Tom Jobim and Vinícius de Moraes saw the stunning *morena* (brunette) who inspired the song named for this bar. Since then, *garotas* have sprung up in every district of Rio.

Balada Sumos (5)

Avenida Ataúlfo de
Paiva, 620 - Leblon
☎ 239 26 99
🕐 Sun.–Thu. 7am–
2am; Fri.–Sat. 7am–
3am; closed Jan. 1,
Shrove Tuesday and
Dec. 25
Serves fruit juices
with unusual
names and flavors.
For a pleasant
surprise, try an
açai, a *fruta do
conde*, or a mixture
of orange and
acerola, depending
on the season. ★
Take the edge off
your hunger with
one of the house
specialties (*pastel*
and *quindim*).

Bar Braca-rense (6)

Rua José Linhares,
85-B - Leblon
☎ 294 35 49
🕐 Mon.–Sat.
7am–1am;
Sun. 9.30am–8pm
Traditional *pé sujo*
(literally 'dirty
foot', a kind of
popular bar)
in Leblon,
frequented by
intellectuals and
local families.
Serves one of the
best *chopes* in Rio,
which you drink
standing at the
counter or at
one of the small
marble tables
on the sidewalk
(*calçada*) outside.

Caneco 70 (7)

Avenida Delfim
Moreira, 1026 -
Leblon
☎ 294 11 80
🕐 Daily 11am–
2am
At the end of
Leblon beach, this
bar was a haunt
of the beautiful
people of the
1970s. The name
is a reference to
the Brazilians'
1970 World Cup
victory, following
earlier wins in
1958 and 1962.
Terrace restaurant
upstairs.

Barraca do Pepê (8)

Avenida do Pepê,
1276 -
Barra da Tijuca
☎ 348 86 08
🕐 Daily 9.30am–
7pm
Trendy Rio
rendezvous
serving
sandwiches with
wonderful fillings.
Large, unpolluted
beach, though
somewhat off the
beaten track. You
may well come
across young
télénovela
actresses and
body builders
showing
themselves off.

Forget your dreams of enjoying a drink at an old wooden or zinc bar counter. That is not the way things are done. You drink your beer *estupidamente gelada* (ice cold, which denotes quality) standing on the sidewalk, or in a traditional *botequim* with ceramic tiles, or out of the heat in a plush, air-conditioned saloon.

After dark

Bar Luiz (9)
Rua da Carioca, 39 - Centro ☎ 262 69 00

🅼 *Carioca* 🕐 *Mon.–Sat. 11am–midnight; closed Dec. 25* ▭

Meeting place of artists and intellectuals, this 100-year-old bar has survived all the upheavals of the city center. It is still invaded every lunch time and evening by a loyal clientele of Cariocas, who quench their thirst with its top-quality *chope*.

Academia da Cachaça (10)
Rua Conde de Bernadotte, 26 - Leblon ☎ 239 15 42

🕐 *Mon. 5pm–2am; Tues.–Sun. noon–2am; closed Dec. 25* ▤

This bar attracts a lot of young people. It serves a wide range of *cachaças* (spirit derived from sugar cane) from all parts of Brazil.★ The more refined of them are well worth trying. Other specialties are *caipirinhas* (*cachaça* and lemon) and *batidas* (*cachaça* and fruit juice), to which you can add condensed milk. But don't overdo it!

Hipódromo (11)
Praça Santos Dumont, 108 - Gávea ☎ 274 97 20

🕐 *Daily 8am–1am; closed Jan. 1, Dec. 25, Wed. of Carnival* ▭

Classic rendezvous of trendy young people from the Zona Sul (in the early evening). You may come across a fashionable artist or two.

Sobre as Ondas (12)
Avenida Atlântica , 3432 - Copacabana ☎ 522 12 16

🅿 🍴 🕐 *Daily 6pm–3am* ● 🚭 🏧 ♿

They certainly know how to concoct a caipirinha! The dance-floor inside attracts bossa-nova enthusiasts.★ From the first floor, there is a good view of the Avenida Atlântica, a craft market and the Ocean. There is also a pleasant terrace.

Not forgetting
■ **Blue Angel (13)** Rua Júlio de Castilhos, 15-B - Copacabana ☎ 570 46 00 *Bar with sophisticated décor. You pay a large amount to get in. The clientele consists of show business personalities and celebrities from the world of culture.*
■ **Caroline Café (14)** Rua J.-J. Seabra, 10 - Jardim Botânico ☎ 540 07 05 *The décor, consisting of American advertising material from the 1950s, is reminiscent of some bars in New York. A late-night rendezvous for fashionable Cariocas. The first-floor terrace is particularly pleasant, the place to try a highly refreshing frozen margarita.*
■ **Quiosque Árabe de Lagoa (15)** Parque Brigadeiro Faria Lima, s/n - Gávea *On a lovely warm evening, go on a gastronomic tour of the various kiosks which surround the Lagoa: be sure to stop off at the Arab kiosk.*

São Cristóvão Zona Portuária

Centro 15
9

Maracanã

Rio Comprido Santa Tereza

Flamengo

Baía de Guanabará

PARQUE NACIONAL DA TIJUCA

Botafogo

PÃO DE AÇÚCAR

Lagoa 14

11 15

Copacabana

10 Leblon 12

Ipanema 13

Oceano Atlântico

N

10

14

13

Bar Luir

9

10

9

53

The hotter it gets, the more Rio comes to life. There are spontaneous outbursts of music in bars and on café terraces, and public concerts are organized at the beach. Spectators are quick to join in, singing and dancing to all the old favorites. In public places, the tables are cleared away to make room for dancing when the mood is right.

After dark

Canecão (16)
Avenida Venceslau Brás, 215 - Botafogo ☎ 543 12 41

M *Botafogo* P ⊘ *ticket office: daily 10am–10pm; performances: Fri.–Sat. 10.30pm Sun. 9pm ● R$ 15-40* ⊟

For thirty years this venue has been a temple of MPB. Chico Buarque, Caetano Veloso, Gal Costa, Djavan, Gilberto Gil and João Bosco have all performed here since their early days, and continue to appear. The friendly, good-natured audience manage to dance, despite the tables and chairs.

Teatro Rival (17)
Rua Álvaro Alvim, 33 - Centro ☎ 240 44 69 ➡ 240 97 96

⊘ *Jan. 3–Dec. 19: Mon.–Sat. 7–9.30pm ● R$ 20–25* ⊟ ⊠

A former cabaret dating from the 1930s, this engaging venue is the reference point for Brazilian music in the city center, just a short walk from the excitement of Cinelândia. Live recordings are often made here, because of the popular, varied program.

Metropolitan (18)
Shopping Via Parque, Avenida Ayrton Senna, 3000 - Barra da Tijuca ☎ 421 13 31 ➡ 385 05 22

P ⊘ *performances: Mon.–Thu. 9.30pm; Fri.–Sat. 10.30pm; Sun. 8.30pm ● R$ 20–190*

Though out of town, this is an obligatory venue for Brazilian musicians, and other stars touring South America. The acoustics are excellent and the modular hall can hold up to 10,500 people. A temple of show business, impressive in both size and professional organization.

Mistura Fina (19)
Avenida Borges de Medeiros, 3207 - Lagoa ☎ 537 28 44

P ▨ ⊘ *Jan. 1–Dec. 23: daily noon–3am. ● R$ 20–47 You must spend at least R$ 12 on drinks* ⊟ ⊞

Beside the Lagoa, upstairs the Mistura Fina runs an excellent jazz and Latin-American music club, which attracts a knowledgeable clientele. ★ You can dine on the pleasant veranda, attend the concert, then go downstairs for a nightcap in the piano bar. Performers here include Dionne Warwick, Michel Legrand and Lenny Andrade.

Not forgetting

■ **Hipódromo Up (20)** Praça Santos Dumont, 108 - Gávea ☎ 294 00 95 *Opened only recently, the first floor of the Hipódromo restaurant stages concerts by well-known Brazilian musicians and young hopefuls.*
■ **Vinícius Piano Bar (21)** Rua Vinícius de Moraes, 39 - Ipanema ☎ 523 47 57 *Meeting place for lovers of jazz, bossa-nova and popular Brazilian music, in plush surroundings.*
■ **Cabeça Feita (22)** Rua Barão da Torre, 665 - Ipanema ☎ 239 30 45 *Young and laid back; eclectic revivals of Brazilian classics.*

Cariocas dine late, go out late and go to bed even later. Rio's night life is rich and varied. There is no lack of choice, from the rock temples of the Zona Sul to the *gafieiras* of the central district. These are traditional dance halls, where couples dance the samba, in the time-honored way, to the sound of a big brass band.

After dark

Gafieira Estudantina (23)

Praça Tiradentes, 79 - Centro
☎ 232 11 49
🕙 Thu. 10.30pm–3.30am; Fri.–Sat. 11pm–4am

One of the last remaining great *gafieiras* in the city center. The repertoire includes the rumba and couples dancing the samba to the music of a band that would have made Glenn Miller green with envy. ★ Pay a visit, if only to watch the star pupils of the ballroom dancing schools, who often perform here.

Lapa (24)

Arco da Velha (samba)
Praça Cardeal Câmara, 132
🕙 Tue.–Sat. 6pm–3am

Asa Branca (forró)
Avenida Mem de Sá, 17
☎ 224 23 42
🕙 Wed. 8pm–3am; Thu.–Sat. 10pm–6am

Fundição Progresso (techno)
Rua dos Arcos, 24-50
☎ 220 50 70
🕙 Fri.–Sat. from 11pm

Not far from the Arcos da Lapa. Here inhabitants of the wealthy Zona Sul rub shoulders with the working classes of the Zona Nord. There is a wide range of music, including *batucada* (percussion), techno, the *forró* style of the Nordeste region, and samba. Casual clothing *de rigueur*.

Feira Nordestina (25)

Campo de São Cristóvão (beneath the entrance ramp of the Linha Vermelha)
🕙 open continuously from Sat. 4pm until Sun. 3pm

This market, vibrant with life from Saturday afternoon until Sunday afternoon, is the meeting place of Rio's Nordeste community. Wander among the Pernambouc hammocks and stalls selling *carne seca* (dried meat), until you find noisy crowds of workers from Nordeste province dancing to the music of *forró* bands. ★ You can be sure of a novel experience, but don't go alone.

Rua Visconde Silva, 13/22 (26)

This street has recently found new life as the meeting place of a growing gay

population. The street and its bars (Jumping Jack and The Must, Queen Victoria and Loch Ness) warm up after midnight.

Rua Pacheco Leão (27)

Public & Co (nº 780)
☎ 239 51 71
2ⁿᵈ Floor (nº 724)
☎ 239 21 91
This small street beside the Jardim Botânico wakes up and puts on its summer clothing at the time of the first heat waves. At night the bars and night clubs attract surfers and crowds of young people from the better-class areas.

El Turf (28)

Jóquei Clube, Praça Santos Dumont, 31 - Gávea
☎ 274 14 44
🕒 Tue.–Sat. 9pm–5am
Young and sophisticated, El Turf offers an all-night program of dancing and international hits. View from the terrace of the illuminated façade of the Jóquei Clube.

Ball-Room (29)

Rua Humaitá, 110 - Humaitá
☎ 537 76 00
🕒 Tue.–Sun. 9pm–4am
This place puts on a highly successful

mixture of pagode concerts (Tue.), forró bands (Thu.) and live rehashes of British and American classics of the 1970s and 1980s (Fri. and Sat.). Switched on student audience.

Hippopotamus (30)

Rua Barão da Torre, 354 - Ipanema
☎ 247 03 51
🖵 🍴 🕒 Tue.–Sun. 8.30pm–4.30am
Private club, fussy about who it lets in. You may not be able to rub shoulders with the celebrities on the dance floor, but you could have more luck with the restaurant.

Rock-In-Rio Café (31)

Barrashopping
➡ 102, Avenida das Américas, 4666 Barra da Tijuca
☎ 431 95 00
🕒 Daily noon–5am
● concerts R$ 10 (women), R$ 12 (men); minimum food charge R$17 🖵
A recently opened venue devoted to rock music. It features some extraordinary metallic décor on an urban theme. Thursday is the day when the young and beautiful cool it to music presented by a superstar DJ. Very popular at weekends.

Dancing the samba is a real challenge. But once you get a feel for this rousing music, you get carried away by the rhythm and general good humor and are soon enjoying yourself. People dance the samba in *gafieiras* and, of course, in samba 'schools'. These *escolas* are really working-class clubs, often near Rio's favelas, where the locals gather

After dark

Casa da Mãe Joana (32)
Rua São Cristóvão, 73 - São Cristóvão ☎ 580 56 13

🔘 *Bossa-nova, MPB* Thu. 9.30pm–3am *Chorinho, Samba de raiz* Sat. 9.30pm–3am ● concert R$ 6 🔲 🈲

The inmates of this former brothel (built in 1803) would have enjoyed the favors of the emperor's entourage. An enthusiastic, lively public now dances to the rhythms of the celebrated *sambistas* who perform at this authentic, popular *gafieira*.

Estação Primeira da Mangueira samba school (33)
Rua Visconde de Niterói, 1072 - Mangueira ☎ 567 46 37

🅿 🔘 *Aug.–Feb. (Carnival): Sat. 11pm–4am* ● R$ 10 🈲

The most popular of Rio's samba schools, founded in 1929, stands at the foot of the favela of Mangueira. It is famous throughout Brazil. There is a boutique selling T-shirts, watches and caps in the green and pink colors of the school. In 1998, Mangueira paid homage to composer and singer Chico Buarque de Hollanda, taking his life and work as the theme of its float.

Acadêmicos do Salgueiro samba school (34)
Rua Silva Teles, 104 - Andaraí ☎ 238 55 64

🔘 *Aug.–Feb. (Carnival): 11pm–4am* ● R$ 10 (women), R$ 15 (men) 🈲

The red and white flags of Salgueiro have always featured prominently in Rio's Carnival. Its supporters, who include many celebrities from artistic and sporting circles (Romário, Edmundo), meet at the *quadra* to sing and dance. At the final rehearsals prior to the Carnival itself, *passistas*, *bahianas* and *mulatas* demonstrate quite exceptional ardor and enthusiasm..

Imperatriz Leopolinense samba school (35)
Rua Profesor Lacê, 235 ☎ 270 80 37 ou 560 80 37

🔘 *Aug.–Feb. (Carnival): 11pm–4am* ● R$ 1 🈲

Carnival winners two years running, in 1994 and 1995, this school has competed no less than 37 times. Its green and white costumes, or *fantasias*, are always breathtaking, and it is also famous for its *bateria* and *ala do tamborim* (drumming contingent).

Not forgetting

■ **Unidos de Vila Isabel samba school (36)** Rua Visconde de Santa Isabel, 34 ☎ 576 70 52 *The blue and white colors of this school have been a source of inspiration to composers Noel Rosa and Martinho de Vila, both from this district with a strong musical tradition.* ■ **União da Ilha samba school (37)** Estrada do Galeão, 332 ☎ 396 49 51 *Near the airport. For its 1998 display this school drew on the life of anthropologist Pierre Verger.* ■ **Helênico (38)** Rua Itapiru, 1305 - Rio Comprido ☎ 502 64 48 *Sports club which organizes dances on Friday evenings and Saturday afternoons. Pagode-style music.*

to dance and prepare for the Carnival procession ➡ 60.

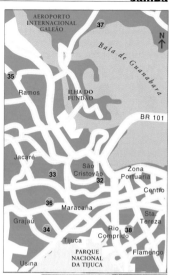

38
34

32

34

34

32

Although only Shrove Tuesday is a public holiday, life stops in Rio for the duration of the Carnival, from the previous Saturday until Ash Wednesday. Cariocas who have not fled the city will attend local festivals and the fancy dress balls organized by the clubs, and may parade with a *bloco*, a *banda* or a samba school. But do not imagine the whole city is in ferment. You need

After dark

Carnival

Supporting a samba school is like supporting a football club. Each school is organized around its **quadra** (headquarters, often at the foot of a favela), where preparations for the Carnival parade go on all the year round. The **carnavalesco**, who acts as producer, choreographer and costume designer, creates a fabulous spectacle involving 3,000 to 4,000 dancers based on current events or a theme from Brazilian history. From August to October, each school organizes a public competition between its composers. The chosen samba is taken up during the **ensaios** (rehearsals), which continue until Carnival time, to the rhythm of the **bateria** (percussion ensemble). Meanwhile, the **carros alegóricos** (floats up to 33 ft high) are built in great secrecy in the school's **barracão** (workshop), and work proceeds on the **fantasias** (costumes). The dancers must buy their costumes (which can cost up to R$ 500). When Carnival arrives, the 18 top schools (**grupo especial**) perform in the **sambódromo** on the nights of Saturday and Sunday, unleashing a colorful tide of joyous celebration. First comes a perfectly choreographed **comissão de frente**, then the **mestre-sala** and **porta-bandeira**, a couple elegantly competing to present the school's flag, then the **bahianas**, older women harmoniously dancing in long swirling dresses. They are followed by the other **alas** (groups of dancers) and the **bateria**, not forgetting the majestic floats carrying **destacas** (the richest decorations) and **passistas** (beautiful young women wearing only the bare essentials). A jury awards marks to each school, following strict and extremely complex criteria. The very best are entitled to a lap of honor during the parade of champions the following Saturday night. The parade of the schools in the *grupo especial*, which attracts all the media attention, is only the tip of the iceberg. The schools in other groups (A, B, C and D) also parade during Carnival, and the best of them will be promoted to the premier division the following year. It is also possible to parade in a local **bloco** or a **banda**, whose improvised costumes can be quite charming (ask when these events are being held). The best known are 'Simpatia é quase amor', 'Suvaco do Cristo' and 'Banda de Ipanema'. Unbeatable atmosphere.
In the golden days of grand balls, the cream of Rio society would meet at the Teatro Municipal ➡ 70 and the Copacabana Palace ➡ 18, all dressed up for the occasion. This tradition has lost some of its appeal, though such dances as the 'Gala gay' at the Scala and 'A night in Bagdad' at the Clube Monte Libano are attempts to perpetuate these somewhat libertine festivals.

Sambódromo (39)
Avenida Marquês de Sapucaí - Cidade Nova

Ⓜ *Praça XI ● between R$ 5 and R$ 180 per evening per person (You can find out where to buy tickets from travel agents or from the receptionist at your hotel)*

Since 1984, the magic of the parade has been focused on the Sambódromo, designed by architect Oscar Niemeyer. More than 70,000 people can crowd onto the terraces, trackside and stands. Avoid sectors 6 and 13, which are set back at the end of the track, allowing only a restricted view.

to find the venues, streets and bars where the action is.

Rua Marquês de Pombal
Rua Benedito Hipólito
R. Frei Caneca
Rua do Paraíso
Avenida ... de ... Março
Pista de Desfile
Praça da Apoteose
Rua Frei Caneca
Rua Pres. Barroso
Av. S de Sá

➡ What to see

Festas Juninas

The popular saints' days (Saint Anthony, Saint John and Saint Peter) are celebrated each year around June 24 throughout Brazil. Even in the city, a village atmosphere prevails. Dances are held in streets decorated with streamers and Chinese lanterns, and people dance the quadrille around blazing bonfires. For the occasion, *baloeiros* (balloon makers) make immense paper balloons, which are filled with hot air and released in the course of the evening.

61

Sights

THE INSIDER'S FAVORITES

According to the popular saying, *Deus criou o mundo em sete dias, mas destes sete só o Rio consumiu dois:* 'God created the world in seven days, but Rio took up two of them'! This is well worth remembering if you are visiting Rio: it takes time to discover the countless riches of this *cidade maravilhosa* – wonderful city.

➡ What to see

Geography

The first surprise in store for the visitor is Rio's spectacular position. Rio de Janeiro (river of January) was so named in January 1502 (or 1504) by the Portuguese who, on glimpsing the entrance to the bay, thought they had discovered a river mouth. The most stunning view of the city and the vast Bay of Guanabara is from the terrace at the foot of the statue of Christ the Redeemer on the Corcovado ('Hunchback mountain', 2,309 ft) ➡ 84. The center of Rio consists of a mountain massif – the Serra da Carioca – around which are arranged the various residential districts. The name derives from the term *acari-oca*, meaning the 'house (or hole) of the fish' in the Tupi Indian language. It was subsequently applied to a river, then the inhabitants of the city (Cariocas). The topography of the city has been radically altered over the years, with spectacular changes taking place, such as the leveling of one of the hills in the Centro district and the filling in of part of the bay.

Districts

To get from the working-class districts of the Zona Nord, where the international airport of Galeão ➡ 8 is located, to the residential districts of the Zona Sul, laid out along the Atlantic beaches ➡ 80, you have to cross the Centro. At the heart of Rio's commercial district lies the Avenida Rio Branco, a spectacular avenue laid out in the early 19th century, feverishly busy on weekdays but practically deserted in the evening and on weekends. You can also get to the Zona Sul via the Rebouças Tunnel (1¾ miles), which passes under the Corcovado. At the entrance to Guanabara Bay stands the Sugar Loaf (1,295 ft) ➡ 84. The oldest districts were laid out on the shores of the bay, and from there the city has gradually spread southward: the Centro district (built in the 17th and 18th centuries) was followed by Flamengo and Botafogo (19th century), then Copacabana (1920s), Ipanema and Leblon (1950s), and more recently São Conrado and Barra (1970s).

Population

According to the most recent census, greater Rio de Janeiro has a population of 11 million. One well-known aspect of this urban sprawl is the existence of favelas (the name derives from an area in the center of the city where veterans of the Canudos campaign squatted in 1897). Official statistics record 573 of these shanty towns, accounting for one fifth of Rio's total population. The favelas of the Zona Sul are the most spectacular, clinging to the *morros* (steep hills) which rise above the urban landscape. Visitors are advised that these areas are dangerous and not easy to get into.

Architecture

Since the beginning of the century, one urban development plan has followed another: new avenues have been laid out, hills and morros leveled, areas of sea and lagoon filled in. Colonial and imperial Rio ➡ 68 was overwhelmed by the developments of the Belle Époque ➡ 70, which did not long resist the implementation of the Agache plan (Agache was a Parisian engineer who settled in Rio in 1926 and was extremely influential as a town-planning consultant). The architecture of the modern movement of the 1930s and 1940s was in turn swept away in the real estate speculation of the 1970s ➡ 72. Rio's Centro district is therefore characterized by a superimposition of architectural layers not sanctioned by any rational zoning policy. To appreciate it, you have to understand the history of the area and take into account the sometimes chaotic clash of period styles.

Further reading

To find out more about Rio, read the stories and novels of Machado de Assis (1839–1908), the city's great naturalist writer: *Epitaph of a Small Winner* or *Philosopher or Dog?*; see Marcel Camus' film *Orfeu Negro* (1959), which won the Palme d'Or at Cannes; and listen to the songs of Antonio Carlos (Tom) Jobim: *Inedito*. The singer Chico Buarque has written a fine novel exploring the city's current ills: *Turbulence* (1992).

In the area

The Praça Quinze is the historic heart of the city. The rapid changes in surrounding areas have for a long time prevented people from appreciating its architectural importance. The city authorities have launched a campaign to revitalize this district, which is a good place for a stroll after office hours.

What to see

Praça Quinze (1)

The square owes its name (XV do Novembro) to the republican coup d'état of November 15, 1889, in which the emperor Dom Pedro II was overthrown. Earlier, on March 7, 1808, it had witnessed the landing of the Portuguese royal family and court – 15,000 people fleeing Lisbon before the advancing armies of Napoleon Bonaparte. It has recently been restored and pedestrianized, making the walk from the Paço Imperial to the landing stage of the Niterói ferry ➡ 84 a great deal more pleasant. On the square stands the former Carmelite convent, now the headquarters of the Cândido Mendes university, beside the Carmelite church, which was begun in 1752 and has been remodeled many times over the years. Next door, the Igreja Ordem Terceira de Nossa Senhora do Monte do Carmo (1754–70) is typical of the carioca baroque style. The portico and nave are painted the traditional white of churches dedicated to the Virgin. In the center of the square is the stone fountain (*chafariz*), which was once on the waterfront, was built by Mestre Valentim (1745–1812), a famous mulatto sculptor.

Paço Imperial (2)
Praça XV de Novembro, 48 - Centro ☎ 533 43 59

Ⓜ *Carioca* Ⓢ *Tues.–Sun. noon–6pm*

Built in 1743 on the foundations of a former warehouse and the Casa de Moeda (Mint), this modest palace was the headquarters of the Portuguese viceroys in colonial times, then the seat of the imperial government until the fall of the dynasty in 1889. However, the emperor preferred to reside in the Quinta da Boa Vista palace ➡ 78. It was from a window of this building that, in 1822, the future emperor Dom Pedro I announced his refusal to rejoin his father, Dom João VI, in Portugal, and this led, on September 7, 1822, to his proclamation of Brazil's independence. Occupied for almost a century by the postal administration, it is now a contemporary art center.

Arco do Teles / Travessa do Comércio (3)

Of the old building that once faced the Paço Imperial all that remains is a section of façade and the arch leading to the Travessa do Comércio. This is one of the most picturesque parts of the city center, its narrow lanes and *sobrados* (two-story buildings) bearing witness to Rio's Portuguese past. The last remaining shipping businesses are fighting a losing battle against the bars, restaurants and art galleries that have invaded the district. The area is very lively on Thursdays and Friday evenings. At the corner of the Rua do Ouvidor, the little Igreja Nossa Senhora da Lapa dos Mercadors (1750), recently restored, has some fine baroque decoration.

Not forgetting

■ **Casa França-Brasil (4)** Rua Visconde de Itaboraí, 78 - Centro ☎ 253 53 66 *French architect Grandjean de Montigny founded the Academy of Fine Arts and, in 1820, erected Brazil's first neoclassical building. Designed as a covered market, for over a century it housed the customs headquarters. Now restored throughout, it stages exhibitions reflecting the cultural links between France and Brazil. Opposite is the Centro Cultural Banco do Brasil ➡ 70.*

Above, a contrast between the 18th and 20th centuries: the Carmelite church and the tower of Cândido Mendes university.

In the area

The narrow streets and colonial palaces which once inspired the painter J.-B. Debret were redeveloped at the end of the 19th century. All that remains are the churches and some vestiges of past glories, such as the Rua do Ouvidor and the Saara district. ■ Where to stay ➡ 24 ■ Where

What to see

Museu Histórico Nacional (5)
Praça Marechal Âncora - Centro ☎ 240 20 92

◯ *Tue.–Fri. 10am–5.30pm; Sat.–Sun. 2–6pm* ● *R$ 3*

This building, of obscure origin, was once an old fort and arsenal. It was rebuilt and enlarged several times until 1922, when it was used as one of the pavilions in the international exhibition celebrating the centenary of Brazil's independence. It is now a museum of Brazilian history. There are fine presentations of the sugar cane, coffee and rubber industries, and documentation on slavery. The museum's collections, totaling more than 30,000 items, include some fascinating curiosities, such as the ivory toys and models once owned by the imperial family.

Mosteiro de São Bento (6)
Rua Dom Gerardo, 68 - Centro ☎ 291 71 22

◯ *Daily 8–11am, 2.30–6pm* **Gregorian chant** *Mon.–Sat. 7.15am, Sun. 10am*

After arriving in Brazil in the late 16th century, the Benedictines built this masterpiece of baroque art on one of Rio's hills. The simple dignity of the façade (1633–41), with its two square bell towers crowned with stone pyramids, contrasts with the vast 18th-century interior, whose walls, side chapels and high altar are richly adorned with gilded wooden sculptures. There are also magnificent silver chandeliers and ceiling paintings dedicated to the Virgin. The monastery's most accomplished sculpture is that of Nossa Senhora de Montserrat, patron saint of the church, which stands near the chapel of the Sacrament, the last on the right before the choir.

Convento de Santo Antônio (7)
Largo da Carioca, s/n - Centro ☎ 262 01 29 ➡ 262 37 72

◯ *Mon., Wed.–Fri. 8am–6pm; Tue. 6am–7.30pm; Sat.–Sun. 9am–5pm*

The Franciscan convent, standing above the urban landscape on the morro of Santo Antônio, was one of the centers of religious power in colonial times. The complex consists of three separate buildings: the convent and its cloister, prolonged by the old prison, now the refectory and library; the simple, towerless church, remodeled several times before it was restored in 1952 by architect Lúcio Costa; and the church of the Ordem Terceira de São Francisco da Penitência. The interior of the last building consists of a magnificent nave paneled in gilded wood, with painted ceilings depicting the glorification of Saint Francis. The three-armed torch-holders beside the altar are of Chinese inspiration. It is possible to visit the church of Santo Antônio, but the church of the Ordem Terceira de São Francisco is closed for the time being.

Not forgetting

■ **Igreja São Francisco de Paula (8)** Largo de São Francisco - Centro ☎ 509 00 67 ◯ *Mon.–Fri. 9am–1pm Many imperial ceremonies were staged here in the 19th century. There are interesting sculptures by Mestre Valentim (chapel of NS da Vitória) and paintings by the slave Manoel da Cunha (Noviciado do Carmo chapel).*

eat ➡ 44 ➡ 46
After dark ➡ 52
Where to shop
110 ➡ 112

Two emperors
ruled over Brazil
in the 19th century:
Dom Pedro I
(1822–31) and
Dom Pedro II
(1831–89).

ILHA DAS
COBRAS

Baía de Guanabara

Avenida do Acre
Rua Dom Gerardo
Avenida Presidente
Av. Marechal Floriano
R. Visc. Inhaúma
Rua Teófilo Otoni
Av. Pres. Vargas
Praça Pio X
R. dos Andradas
Rua da Alfândega
Rua de Buenos Aires
Rua do Rosario
Rua do Ouvidor
L. de S. Francisco
Rua 7 de Setembro
Rua da Assembléia
Rua da Carioca
Av. Nilo Peçanha
Carioca
Av. Rep. do Chile
Avenida Almirante Barroso
Rua México
Rua Debret
Av. Pres. A. Carlos
R. Mal. Aguilnado
Av. E. Braga
Pr. XV
Pr. Rui Barbosa
Kubitschek
Rio de Janeiro
Rua do Branco
Rua Uruguaiana

69

In the area

At the end of the 19th century, Rio experienced a time of radical change. Survivors from this period are the neo-gothic turquoise palace on the Ilha Fiscal, the buildings around Tiradentes square, and the amazing Confeitaria Colombo… ■ Where to stay ➡ 24 ■ Where to eat ➡ 44 ➡ 46

What to see

Avenida Rio Branco (9)

On the pretext of improving living conditions in the district, where yellow fever was rife, in 1904–5 'builder-mayor' Pereira Passos opened up the 'Avenida Central', a development inspired by Baron Haussmann's new boulevards in Paris. It was subsequently named the Rio Branco. A design competition was held for the new buildings, of which only a few examples, such as the Clube Naval, have survived. They can be seen in the vicinity of Floriano square (known as 'Cinelândia' because of the many cinemas once concentrated there). The new traffic artery created a permanent separation between the north of the city, with its industries, harbor and working-class districts, and the more fashionable Zona Sul.

Teatro Municipal (10)
Praça Floriano - Centro ☎ 544 29 00

Ⓜ *Cinelândia* 🕒 *Mon.–Fri. 9am–5pm* 🎟 ● *guided tour R$ 2*

There is no hiding the French ancestry of this building, inaugurated on July 14, 1909. It was built between 1902 and 1906 by architect Francisco Pereira Passos, who borrowed some of his ideas from Charles Garnier's Paris Opera. The season is no longer as brilliant as in the days of Sarah Bernhardt and Toscanini, but the program is still worth studying. On the ground floor of the theater, on the Rio Branco side, is the entrance to the Assírio restaurant ➡ 46, with its extravagant neo-Babylonian décor.

Museu Nacional de Belas Artes (11)
Avenida Rio Branco, 199 - Centro ☎ 240 00 68 ➡ 262 60 67

Ⓜ *Cinelândia* 🕒 *Tue.–Fri. 10am–6pm; Sat.–Sun. 2–6pm* ● *R$ 4, free on Sun.*

The museum was installed in 1908 in a building also designed to house the School of Fine Arts, which in 1976 transferred to the campus of the federal university. The main gallery is devoted to 19th-century Brazilian artists: members of the French mission of 1816 such as Nicolas Antoine Taunay (1755–1830); Brazil's two greatest historical painters, Vitor Mereiles (1832–1903) and Pedro Américo (1843–1905), whose gigantic *Batalha do Avaí* is on show; and, in a quite different vein, the impressionist Eliseu Visconti. Also of interest is the imperial family's Italian collection (16th–18th centuries). The 20th-century gallery provides a good introduction to modern and contemporary Brazilian art.

Not forgetting

■ **Around Praça Tiradentes (12)** *The hub of artistic life in the late 19th century, with its theaters and cabarets. Note the Real Gabinete Português de Leitura and the steel construction of the Iris cinema in Rua da Carioca.* ■ **Biblioteca Nacional (13)** *Avenida Rio Branco, 219 - Centro ☎ 262 82 55* 🎟 *Mon.–Fri. 11am, 3pm, 5pm The largest national library in Latin America. Its nucleus was the royal library imported from Lisbon in 1808* ■ **Casa Cavé (14)** *Rua 7 de Setembro, 133 - Centro ☎ 221 05 33* 🕒 *Mon.–Fri. 9am–7pm; Sat. 9am–1pm This traditional tearoom, opened in 1860 and remodeled in Art-Deco style in 1920, gives a feel for what Rio was like in the Belle Époque* ■ **Centro Cultural Banco do Brasil (15)** *Rua Primero de Março, 66 - Centro ☎ 216 02 37* 🕒 *Tue.–Sun. noon–8pm The bank's former head office is now a major cultural center (theaters, art and experimental cinema, video room, exhibition areas, bookshop).*

■ After dark
➡ 52 ➡ 54 ➡ 56
■ Where to shop
➡ 110 ➡ 112

ILHA DAS COBRAS

Baía de Guanabara

Av.Marechal Floriano
Rua do Acre
Avenida R.Dom Gerardo
Rua Teófilo Otoni
R.Visc.Inhaúma
Praça Pio X
Av.Pres.Vargas
Rua Buenos Aires
Avenida Passas
Avenida do Paraguai
Uruguaiana
Rua do Rosario
Rua do Ouvidor
Rua da Assembléia
Rua da Carioca
Rua 7 de Setembro
Av.Rio Branco
Av.Pres. A. Carlos
Av.E.Braga
Av.Presidente Kubitschek
Mal.Aguilnado
Carioca
Av.Rep. do Chile
Av. Almirante Barroso
Nilo Peçanha
Av. General Justo
Graça Aranha
Luzia
Av.Churchill
Av.F.Roosevelt
Cinêlandia
Pr. do Monroe
Av.Pres.Wilson
Av.Beira Mar
Pr. Itália
Lg.da Lapa
Santa

Nineteenth-
century
architecture
in Rio was
influenced
by the neo-
Manuélin style in
Portugal and by
contemporary
trends in Paris.

It is easy to underestimate the 20th century's contribution to Rio's architectural development. Yet Brazil's former capital has been a proving ground for architects and town planners, with buildings by Le Corbusier, Agache, Lúcio Costa, Reidy, Niemeyer and others. ■ Where to stay ➡ 24

What to see

Palácio Gustavo Capanema (16)
Rua da Imprensa, 16 - Centro ☎ 220 07 39 ➡ 220 14 89

Ⓜ *Cinelândia* ◐ *Mon.–Fri. 9am–6pm*

Designed in 1936 by a team of young architects who, twenty years later, were to plan Brasília (Lúcio Costa, Oscar Niemeyer, Affonso Reidy), this building was erected to house the Ministry of Education and Health, with the encouragement of the forward-looking minister Capanema. The 16-story structure, with its piles, sun screen and open-plan office space, was influenced by the drawings of Franco-Swiss architect Le Corbusier, who twice visited Rio (1929 and 1936). The decoration was entrusted to the best artists of the period, in particular Portinari, who was responsible for the *azulejos* on the ground floor and the frescos on the second. To visit the building, apply for a pass at reception.

Museu de Arte Moderna (17)
Avenida Infante Dom Henrique, 85 - Centro ☎ 210 21 88

Ⓜ *Cinelândia* ◐ *Tues.–Sun. noon–6pm* ● *R$ 5*

Designed by Affonso Eduardo Reidy and begun in 1955, the museum is on two levels, 426 ft long by 82 ft wide, supported by a series of reinforced concrete arches, with no internal pillars. It was ravaged by fire in 1978, which destroyed a large part of the international collections and caused irreparable damage to a retrospective of work by painter Torres Garcia. Thanks to the generosity of collectors and artists, and the solidarity of institutions in other countries, the museum has risen from the ashes. It houses the Gilberto Chateaubriant collection, the most important collection of contemporary Brazilian art.

Parque do Flamengo (18)

This 296-acre park was created in the 1960s, when it became necessary to build an expressway between the Centro and the Zona Sul. The land was reclaimed from the bay, between Santos Dumont airport and Botafogo beach, and planted with Brazilian and exotic species of trees and shrubs by Burle Marx. The beaches of Flamengo and Botafogo were relocated. A good place for a stroll, the park includes a monument to those killed in the last war, a marina (Marina da Glória), and a museum devoted to the singer Carmen Miranda (*Avenida Rui Barbosa, 560, open daily*). Motor vehicles are excluded from the area on Sundays.

Not forgetting

■ **Avenida Chile (19)** *This district was created when the Morro Santo Antônio was leveled (1958–60). All that remains of the hill is the rise on which the convent stands. On either side of the avenues of Chile and Paraguay are some impressive buildings: the cathedral (1964–76), which can hold 20,000 worshipers, and the head office of Petrobrás, a cube-shaped building whose balconies conceal hanging gardens* ■ **Edificio Manchete (20)** *Rua do Russell, 804 – Glória Headquarters of the television organization and the weekly magazine Manchete, this is one of the best examples of Oscar Niemeyer's work in Rio* ■ **Parque Guinle (21)** *The park of Palácio Laranjeiras, the governor's residence, is an attempt at a middle-class city garden (1948–54). Lúcio Costa was looking for a synthesis of the Brazilian way of life and modern construction systems.*

■ Where to eat ➡ 42
➡ 44 ➡ 46
■ After dark ➡ 54 ➡ 56
■ What to buy ➡ 112

In the area
Fashionable heart of the city in the 1850s, the Rua do Catete has kept some of its attractive old facades and, by the church, the pump from the the city's old sewage system, which was loaded onto ships and dumped out at sea!
■ Where to stay ➡ 24 ■ Where to eat ➡ 42 ■ Where to shop ➡ 112

What to see

Igreja Nossa Senhora
da Glória do Outeiro (22)
Ladeira Nossa Senhora da Glória, 26 - Glória ☎ 225 28 69

Ⓜ *Glória* Ⓞ *Mon.–Fri 8am–noon, 1–5pm; Sat.–Sun. 8am–noon*

A constant feature of canvases by visiting painters, the small Glória church was a landmark for mariners entering the bay. Built in the early 18th century (1714–19) to an elliptical plan, it consists of two polygons (nave and choir) fitted together to form a figure-of-eight. Attractively simple, with its wooden paneling and *azulejos*, it was restored and equipped with new access ramps by architect Lúcio Costa. Opposite the sacristy is a small museum of sacred art.

Templo da Humanidade (23)
Rua Benjamin Constant, 74 - Glória ☎ 224 38 61

Ⓜ *Glória* Ⓞ *Sun. 10am–1pm*

The positivist religion founded by Auguste Comte found fertile ground in Brazil, where this Temple of Humanity was built in 1897. The weather vane points to Paris. Inside, scientists and famous people are venerated instead of saints. Positivist ideas had a lasting influence on the founders of the republican regime, who chose Comte's motto – *Ordem e Progresso* – to feature on the new national flag.

Museu da República (24)
Rua do Catete, 153 - Glória ☎ 285 63 20

Ⓜ *Catete* Ⓞ *Tue.–Fri. noon–7pm; Sat., Sun., public holidays 2–6pm* ● *R$ 3, free on Wed.* 🎬 **Cinema museum** *(for information, inquire at the museum or call the number given above)*

Built between 1858 and 1866 by a German architect for Baron de Nova Friburgo, the Catete palace became the seat of the republican government in 1897. It was here, on August 24, 1954, that President Getúlio Vargas, first dictator (1930–45) then elected president (1950–4), committed suicide, having failed to resolve a political crisis between the trade unions and the military. His bedroom remains as it was in 1954. In 1960 the palace became a museum. As well as recording the bourgeois splendor of the Brazilian Republic, the museum functions primarily as a research and cultural center (with restaurant, bookshop, theater and multimedia facilities).

Not forgetting
■ **Museu do Folclore Edison Carneiro (25)** Rua do Catete, 181 – Glória ☎ 285 04 41 Ⓞ Tue.–Fri. 11am–6pm; Sat.–Sun. 3–6pm *This fine collection is evidence of the growing interest in popular arts and traditions shown by Brazilian ethnologists (including Edison Carneiro) since the 1950s.*
■ **Café Glória (26)** Rua do Russell, 734 - Glória ☎ 205 96 47
Ⓞ Tue.–Sun. noon–11pm *This splendid café is housed in a former beach villa, built in the most exuberant Art-Nouveau style.*

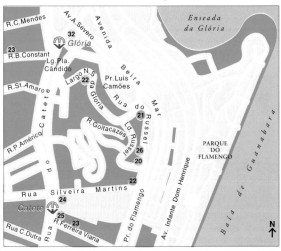

These fine 19th-century façades in the Rua do Catete are now listed buildings.

In the area

Home of artists and the old carioca bourgeoisie, the Santa Tereza district stands on an enchanting hill with many unsuspected attractions. Fine houses, hidden gardens and bistros frequented by local people make it one of Rio's most appealing districts. ■ After dark ➡ 56

What to see

Le Bonde (27)
Rua Professor Lélio Gama, 65 - Centro ☎ 240 57 09

M *Carioca* 🚋 *Streetcar terminus at the above address, opposite the Petrobrás building* 🕐 *Daily 7am–10pm* ● *R$ 0.65*

Last vestige of the days when streetcars linked all parts of the city, the *bonde* (named after its English designer, a Mr Bond, and affectionately known to cariocas as the '*bondinho*') has been negotiating the hill of Santa Tereza for the last hundred years. Listed as a historic monument, the Bonde is a great way to travel, though somewhat precarious with bunches of children hanging on to the running boards.
★ A ride on the little yellow streetcar is the best way to get acquainted with this picturesque district, where favelas coexist with artists' studios and middle-class residences.

Arcos da Lapa (28)

M *Cinelândia*

This old aqueduct (*Aqueduto da Carioca*), constructed between 1744 and 1750, is one of the few civil building projects surviving from the colonial era. It once channeled the waters of the Rio Carioca ➡ 64 from the foot of the Corcovado ➡ 84, via the hill of Santa Tereza, to the Largo da Carioca. In full view since the neighboring buildings were demolished in the 1970s, it serves as a viaduct for the Bonde.

Museu da Chácara do Céu (29)
Rua Murtinho Nobre, 93 - Santa Tereza ☎ 507 19 32

🕐 *Wed.–Mon. noon–5pm* ● *R$ 2* 🌿

Art patron Raymundo de Castro Maya lived in one of the finest properties in Santa Tereza. His villa, built in the 1950s, has been converted into a museum which has works by Vlaminck and Picasso, and a fine collection of water-colors by Jean-Baptiste Debret (1769–1848), a member of the French art mission. They depict the daily life and customs of Brazil during that period. The French mission (1816) was the fruit of an initiative by Dom João VI, who wanted Rio to have educational and cultural facilities based on a European model. ★ From the 'park of ruins', opened in 1997 and just a short walk from the Chácara do Céo (little house in the sky), there is a fine view of Guanabara Bay.

Not forgetting

■ **Centro Cultural Laurinda Santos Lobo (30)** Rua Monte Alegre, 306 - Santa Tereza ☎ 242 97 41 🕐 Mon.–Fri. 10am–6pm; Sat–Sun. noon–5pm *Cultural center housed in one of the finest residences in Santa Tereza.*
■ **Museu Casa de Benjamin Constant (31)** Rua Monte Alegre, 255 - Santa Tereza ☎ 509 12 48 🕐 Thurs.–Sun. 1–5pm *This house was owned by Benjamin Constant de Magalhães, the founder of Positivism in Brazil, who influenced the coup d'état of 1889 (end of the Empire). It is now a museum.*
■ **Convento de Santa Tereza (32)** Ladeira de Santa Tereza - Santa Tereza *Carmelite convent after which the district is named.*

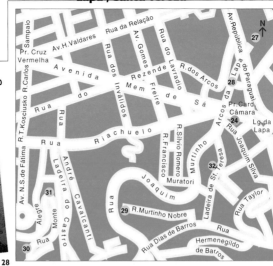

The Arcos, one of Rio's most enduring symbols, are once again in the thick of the city's night life.

In the area

São Cristovão had its heyday in the 19th century. There are many signs of its former splendor, such as the old observatory (museum of astronomy) and the Emperor's bathhouse. ■ Where to eat ➡ 44 ➡ 46 ■ After dark ➡ 52 ➡ 56 ➡ 58 ■ Where to shop ➡ 110 ➡ 112

What to see

Igreja Nossa Senhora da Candelária (33)
Praça Pio X - Centro ☎ 233 23 24

Ⓜ *Uruguaiana* 🕐 *Mon.–Fri. 8am–4pm*

At the busy junction of avenues Presidente Vargas and Rio Branco, the Candelária was Rio's largest church until superseded by the new cathedral. The main body of the building was completed in 1811, but work continued until 1898. In the middle of the square is a cross commemorating a massacre of street children by a death squad in July 1993.

Avenida Presidente Vargas (34)

Almost 2½ miles long and 262 ft wide, this avenue was driven through an existing district in the years 1941 to 1944. The station building (Estação D. Pedro II, but known as 'Central' station), with its 360-ft tower and clock, and the Palácio Duque de Caxias typify a style half way between a North American model and the grandiose architecture of a totalitarian state. Building development has since continued out beyond the Sambódromo ➡ 60. The final block, the *Teleporto*, is a complex of 'intelligent' skyscrapers, billed as the office accommodation of the future.

Palácio do Itamaraty (35)
Museu Histórico e Diplomático, Avenida Marechal Floriano, 196 - Centro ☎ 253 76 91 ➡ 263 30 53

Ⓜ *Presidente Vargas* 🕐 *Mon., Wed., Fri. 1.15–4.15pm* 🎫 *free guided tours*

In 1897 this former residence of the Baron of Itamaraty became the Ministry of Foreign Affairs. Although the ministry transferred to Brasilia in 1960, the palace has kept its former name. With its enclosed patio and swans, it is a haven of tranquility at the heart of a bustling district. The museum of diplomacy, housed in the magnificently restored reception rooms, has a fine collection of old maps.

Quinta da Boa Vista (36)
Museu Nacional - São Cristóvão ☎ 568 82 62

Ⓜ *São Cristóvão* 🕐 *Tues.–Sun. 10am–4pm* ● *R$ 3*

When the royal family landed in Rio in 1808, they were offered this *quinta* (country house) by a wealthy settler. In 1826 it became the imperial residence, and was nicknamed the 'tropical Versailles'. The park (1866–76) was laid out on hilly ground by the French landscape gardener Auguste Glaziou, with tropical flora and an artificial lake. The zoo dates from 1945. The republican government converted the palace into a museum of natural history and ethnology. It has ten million exhibits.

Not forgetting

■ **Campo de Sant'Ana (37)** Praça da República - Centro ☎ 224 15 09 *One of the city's finest parks, laid out by A. Glaziou, where cutias (a species of rodent) are free to roam.* ■ **Museu do Primeiro Reinado (38)** Avenida Pedro II, 293 - Centro ☎ 589 96 27 *Dom Pedro I built this attractive private residence for his mistress, Domitila, Marchioness of Santos.*

The beach is part of daily life in Rio, a 'city within the city'. The cariocas have an irrepressible need to see and be seen, even on the hottest days. Open to all comers, even though the *postos* (lookout posts) tend to form clear boundaries between groups of different social backgrounds.

What to see

Copacabana (39)

With nearly 200,000 inhabitants, the visitor's impression of Copacabana is of a 2¹/₂-mile beach and a single avenue, the Avenida Atlântica, whose sidewalks are adorned with black and white, Portuguese-style paving, redesigned by Roberto Burle Marx in 1970. The image of a Virgin brought from Bolivia was venerated here in the late 19th century. 'Copacabana' means 'blue and sunny beach' in the Quecha Indian language. For many years the beach was difficult to get to, but when two tunnels were dug through the mountain (in 1892 and 1906), people flocked to the area. The first wave of development brought Art-Deco villas and resort-style houses, some of which can still be seen in the side streets. In the 1940s, the original buildings were superseded by a rather unoriginal international style of architecture. In the 1970s, land was reclaimed from the sea to build the present double traffic thoroughfare. The legendary beach is a lively place, with people playing *peladas* and beach volleyball to the rhythm of the samba. The sidewalks are crowded with drinks stands and *camelôs* (pedlars), but the fishermen's cooperative has withstood all these pressures. ★ Fish is sold every day at *posto* 6.

Ipanema / Leblon (40)

Fashions change. In the early 1960s, the middle classes deserted Copacabana in favor of Ipanema. It was the exciting era of the bossa-nova with Tom Jobim and Vinicius de Moraes, who wrote the big international hit *Garota de Ipanema* (*The Girl from Ipanema*). Fashionable boutiques sprang up everywhere and real estate speculation disfigured the sea front, where, in reaction to Copacabana, buildings were limited to four stories. Though it has lost some of its prestige, Ipanema still attracts the young and fashionable. The procession of beach-side joggers is like a fashion parade, and the children of the wealthy have their *point* between *posto* 9 and 10.

São Conrado (41)

Squeezed between sea and mountain, the district of São Conrado is dominated by the impressive Pedra da Gávea. The sky is dotted with the colorful fabrics of hang gliders and parachutes, which land at the far end of the beach. São Conrado is a place of contrasts. The Gávea golf club ➡ 15 is right beside the favela of Rocinha, the largest in Brazil, which clings to the spurs of the Morro dos Dois Irmãos (the two brothers).

Not forgetting

■ **Barra da Tijuca (42)** *Rio's longest beach (11 miles), which is pollution free. The inhabitants of Barra live in enclosed* condomínios, *groups of buildings with tight security arrangements. This is an up-and-coming district. Young people congregate at the Barraca do Pepê* ➡ 51.
■ **Plage de Grumari (43)** *A natural heritage site, Grumari and the neighboring beach of Prainha (a surfers' paradise) are backed by a low mountain planted with bananas. There is a magnificent view from here.*
■ **Barra de Guaratiba (44)** *Twenty-eight miles out of town are two small beaches, accessible on foot, which have remained unspoiled. Here you get a sense of what 16th-century travelers must have felt on first approaching Rio. Visit the Sítio Burle Marx, house of the celebrated landscape artist, with its garden of rare plants.*

N↑

JACAREPAGUÁ

PARQUE NACIONAL
DA TIJUCA

Vargem
Grande   Riocentro

Alto da
Boa Vista

Botafogo   PÃO DE
Lagoa°   AÇÚCAR
            Copacabana

LAGOA
DA TIJUCA

Manhangá

São
Conrado
41

Leblon Ipanema
40

39

Recreio dos
Bandeirantes

Jeá

42 Barra da Tijuca

Oceano Atlântico

44
43
10km /4km

39

39

39

COLÔNIA DE PESCADORES Z.13
PATRIA E DEVER
R.J.

43

Tropical vegetation is a characteristic feature of Rio de Janeiro, the forest reaching right into the heart of the city. The greenery of its many gardens makes it unique among the great cities of the world. Of special interest is the Tijuca national park (8,150 acres), not to be confused with the Floresta (an area of tropical forest within the park, see below) or

What to see

Jardim Botânico (45)
Rua Jardim Botânico, 1008 - Jardim Botânico ☎ 274 48 98

🕒 *Tues.–Sun. 8am–5pm* ● *entrance fee: R$ 2; parking : R$ 2*

While exiled in Rio, Dom João VI created a botanical garden for growing the spices Portugal imported from the East Indies. His efforts formed the nucleus of the Jardim Botânico, covering 338 acres and featuring two types of vegetation: the higher ground is clothed in tropical rain forest, a vestige of the original *mata atlântica* while the botanical garden, in the true sense of the word, has over 6,000 plant species from all over the world. Among the most fascinating plants are the 'sensitives', which close their leaves when touched,the insect eaters, the bromeliads, and the many varieties of orchid. The most characteristic feature of the garden is its avenue of 'imperial' palms.

Floresta de Tijuca (46)
Estrada da Cascatinha, 850 - Alto da Boa Vista ☎ 492 22 53

🕒 *Daily 8am–5pm*

In a former coffee plantation, in the heart of town, this area of tropical forest was replanted by the emperor Dom Pedro II at a time (1857) when uncontrolled tree felling seemed likely to dry up the streams supplying the city's drinking water. Cariocas come here to escape the heat of the central districts. The park is accessible from many parts of town.

Vista Chinesa (47)

Just off the road connecting the Jardim Botânico with the Floresta de Tijuca, this pagoda-style pavilion is one of the best places to view the city and its surroundings: the Corcovado ➡ 84, the Sugar Loaf ➡ 84, Guanabara Bay, the districts of Ipanema and Leblon, and the series of *morros* beyond Niterói ➡ 84.

Paineiras (48)

On weekends, one of the roads through Tijuca national park is closed to traffic, becoming a haven for wildlife and people keeping fit. The road is taken over by hikers, joggers and cyclists, inhaling the scent of the tropical forest. The boldest spirits cool off under waterfalls. ★ Fine views of the various districts of the city. You may catch a glimpse of monkeys and toucans.

Not forgetting

■ **Museu do Açude (49)** Estrada do Açude, 764 - Alto da Boa Vista ☎ 492 21 19 🕒 *Thu.–Sun. 11am–4.30pm This magnificent house was left to the city in 1943 by art patron Raymundo de Castro Maya. Small museum of beautiful azulejos and collection of colonial furniture.* ■ **Parque da Cidade (50)** Estrada Santa Marinha, 505 - Gávea 🕒 *Daily 8am–5.30pm This park, covering 116 acres, contains a museum of the city's history. Fine view of the sea and Leblon beach.* ■ **Parque Lage (51)** Rua Jardim Botânico, 414 ☎ 539 96 24 *Park covering 128 acres, two thirds of it tropical forest. The residence built in 1920 by tycoon Henrique Lage for his Italian opera-star wife now houses the School of Visual Arts.*

the beach of Barra da Tijuca
➡ 80.

Tijuca national park, Rio's green lung, is the largest city park in the world.

On the way to the Corcovado, beside the little mountain railroad station, is a museum of naive art, with an excellent collection of paintings and bookshop. Farther on, the Largo do Boticário, on the Rio Carioca, is a charming group of old houses from the city center, relocated here in the 1940s around a small paved square.

What to see

Pão de Açúcar (52)

🚡 Cable car (bondinho) leaving from Avenida, 520 - Praia Vermelha
☎ 541 37 37 🕐 Daily 8am–10pm (every 30 mins) ● R$ 15.50 ♿

Standing guard over Guanabara Bay, the Sugar Loaf is probably Rio's most celebrated sight. From the top (1,295 ft), there is an impressive view of the bay, the twin towns of Niterói and Rio, the bridge connecting them, the beaches and the Atlantic Ocean. It is flanked by two other morros: the Urca and the Cara de Cão ('dog face'). You reach the top by a two-stage cableway, total length 4,265 ft. The lower station, Morro da Urca (721 ft) is sometimes open in the evenings.

Morro do Corcovado (53)

🚗 By road through Tijuca national park 🚃 By train from Rua Cosme Velho, 513
(☎ 558 13 29) 🕐 Daily 9am–6pm (every 30 mins) ● R$ 15

The 'Hunchback mountain' (2,310 ft) was a popular tourist attraction even before the erection of Carlos Oswald's statue of Christ the Redeemer which, made of concrete, stands 98 ft high. The head and hands were modeled by Paul Landowsky. It was originally planned to mark the hundredth anniversary of Brazilian independence (1922) but, due to a shortage of funds, it was not inaugurated until October 12, 1931, by the dictator Getúlio Vargas.

Praia Vermelha / Morro da Urca (54)

Starting point: Cláudio Coutinho track (on the Praia Vermelha) open daily until 5pm. At the 300m (328 yds) mark, take the first path into the forest on your left. When you reach the ridge, turn left toward the intermediate station of the Sugar Loaf cableway (Morro da Urca) or right to reach the foot of the rockface ♿

Although rock-climbing on the Corcovado or Sugar Loaf is strictly for experienced, properly equipped mountaineers, anyone can enjoy an hour's hike on the Morro da Urca, and appreciate one of the finest views of the bay, without getting hopelessly lost.

Niterói (55)

⛴🕐 Aerobarco (hydrofoil) from the Praça XV Mon.–Fri. 6.30am–8pm (every 30 mins) Ferry Daily 5.30am–10.30pm Museu de Arte Contemporânea Mirante de Boa Viagem ☎ 620 24 00 🕐 Tue.–Fri., Sun. 11am–7pm; Sat. 1–9pm ● R$ 3 @ macnit@urbi.com.br ♿

A city of 450,000 people located on the opposite side of the bay, Niterói is linked to Rio by an 8¾-mile road bridge. It is generally neglected by tour operators. The opening in 1996 of the Museu de Arte Contemporânea, a great concrete flower of a building designed by Oscar Niemeyer offering an extraordinary view of Rio, should redress the balance.

■ Ilha de Paquetá (56) Landing Stage Praça XV - The most beautiful island in the bay is unusual in shape: two areas of higher ground linked by an isthmus at which boats land their passengers. Its beaches, with their almost spherical rocks, have attracted many artists.

Map labels: N, 56, AEROPORTO INTERNACIONAL GALEÃO, Moneró, Freguesia, Ribeira, Pto Novo, Ramos, ILHA DO FUNDÃO, BR 101, Neves, Barreto, Baía de Guanabara, São Cristovão, Centro, NITERÓI, Gragoatá, 55, Icaraí, Sta. Tereza, Tijuca, Flamengo, Jurujuba, Usina, PARQUE NACIONAL DA TIJUCA, 53, Botafogo, 52, 54, Lagoa, Copacabana, Ipanema, Oceano Atlântico, São Conrado

53

Rio is so lush and green, you can enjoy many
excursions without leaving the city limits!

55

53

54

53

If you get the chance, go to a match between two of the big carioca clubs, for a spectacular display of popular enthusiasm, flag-waving, brass bands and singing, in a generally good-natured atmosphere. It is best to buy tickets ahead at the stadium, or through one of the clubs involved.

What to see

Maracanã (57)
Rua Professor Eurico Rebello (porte 18) - Maracanã ☎ 568 99 62

Visits 🕐 *Mon.–Fri. 9am–5p; Sat.–Sun. 9am–3pm except on match days* ● *R$ 4*
Matches generally on Wed. and Sun. evenings

Inaugurated in 1950 to host the only World Cup competition yet played in Brazil, the Maracanã stadium was on that occasion packed with 200,000 spectators, who watched Brazil lose to Uruguay (2–1), a disaster which still lives on in the carioca collective memory. But the stadium has also known its days of glory. It was here that Edson Arantes do Nascimento, known to the world as 'Pelé', scored his thousandth goal (1969) playing for Santos Futebol Clube from the state of São Paolo. For safety reasons, the stadium's capacity has been reduced to 122,386 places. Three major tournaments are played here: the Torneio Rio-São Paolo, the Campeonato Brasileiro and the Campeonato Carioca.

Clube de Regatas do Flamengo (58)
Av. Borges de Medeiros, 997 - Leblon ☎ 529 01 00

🕐 *Daily 7am–10pm* @ *http://www.flamengo.com.br*

Originally founded in 1895 as a rowing club, Flamengo converted to football in 1912. Nicknamed Rubro-Negro (from the red and black of the team jerseys), the club of Zico and Romário is the most popular in Rio. The highly organized *torcida* (the supporters' club has 22,000 registered members) is a spectacle in its own right.

Fluminense Football Club (59)
Rua Alvaro Chaves, 41 - Laranjeiras ☎ 553 72 40

🕐 *Mon.–Fri. 24 hours; Sat.–Sun. 7am-6pm* @ *http://www.fluminense.esp.br*

Founded in 1902, Fluminense was responsible for building Brazil's first football stadium. Originally a cricket club, it has maintained a more aristocratic approach to the game than its rivals. Housed in a fine building with stained-glass windows in the residential district of Laranjeiras, 'Flu' still enjoys great prestige (17,000 members), though demoted to the 3rd division in 1998.

Clube Botafogo de Futebol e Regatas (60)
Rua Venceslau Brás, 72 - Botafogo ☎ 543 72 72

🕐 *Daily 9am–6pm* @ *http://www.botafogo.com.br*

Long in the doldrums, Botafogo is now on the up and up: Brazilian champions in 1995, Carioca Cup winners in 1997, the club has suddenly become popular. Its slogan: 'A passion which goes beyond reason.'

Club de Regatas Vasco da Gama (61)
Rua General Almério de Moura, 131 - São Cristovão ☎ 580 73 73

🕐 *Daily 8am–7pm* @ *http://www.crvasco.com.br*

Founded in 1898 (400th anniversary of the discovery of the Indies), this club converted to football in 1916. Very popular with the Portuguese community: Romário made his debut here; Bebeto and Edmundo were former stars.

61 São Cristóvão, Zona Portuária, Centro
57 Maracanã, Rio Comprido, Santa Tereza, Flamengo
59
60 Botafogo, PÃO DE AÇÚCAR
Lagoa
Copacabana
58 Leblon, Ipanema
PARQUE NACIONAL DA TIJUCA
Baía de Guanabara
Oceano Atlântico

N

Avenida Bartolomeu de Gusmão
Maracanã
DERBY CLUB
Avenida Presidente Castelo Branco
Praça Pres. Emílio Garrastazu Médici
Estádio Célio de Barros
Estádio Mário Filho
57 Parque Aqu1atico Júlio de Lamare
COMPLEXO ESPORTIVO DO MARACANÃ
Ginásio Gilberto Cardoso
Rua Mata Machado
Av. Prof. M. de Abreu
R. São Francisco Xavier
Rua Prof. Eurico Rabelo
R.A. Meneses
R.I. de Figueiredo
Avenida Maracanã
Av. P. Sousa

61 CRVG CBF BRASIL

57

60

59

58

Air travel

The quickest way to reach Belo Horizonte ➡ 98 (255 miles) is by air from Santos Dumont airport ➡ 8.

➡ Further afield

Bus services

There are regular services, leaving from one of the estações rodoviárias (bus stations).

Terminal Rodoviária Novo Rio ➡ 8
Avenida Francisco Bicalho, 1 - Santo Cristo
☎ *291 51 51* Departures for all major towns.

Distances

Rio de Janeiro is a good base for exploring the Atlantic coastline, the old imperial towns (Petrópolis and Teresópolis ➡ 94) and the historic towns of the Minas Gerais. But remember that Brazil is a big country. It takes four hours to get to Paraty by road, five to Tiradentes. The nearest destination, Petrópolis, is one hour from Rio.

12

Excursions

THE INSIDER'S FAVORITES

Dates of local festivals

Jan. 1 *Procissão Marítima* (Angra dos Reis ➡ 92)
Jan. 6 *Folia de Reis* (Paraty ➡ 92)
Holy Saturday *Proussão da Resureição* (Ouro Prêto ➡ 98)
Weekend before Pentecost *Festa do Divino* (Paraty ➡ 92)

All the bus services listed below leave from Rio's Rodavíaria Novo Rio ➡ 8. From Belo Horizonte, several bus companies run regular services to the towns of Ouro Prêto, Mariana and Congonhas. (*Belo Horizonte bus terminal* ☎ *(031) 271 30 00*)

➡ Further afield

Paraty (1)

157 miles southwest of Rio
🚌 (3½ hrs) BR-101 as far as Paraty
🚌 (4 hrs) Cie Costa Verde
☎ 233 38 09
● R$ 16.94

Angra dos Reis (2)

94 miles southwest of Rio
🚌 (2¼ hrs) BR 101 (follow signs to Santos) as far as Angra dos Reis
🚌 (2hrs 20 mins) Cie Costa Verde
☎ 233 38 09
● R$ 11.91

Búzios (3)

110 miles northeast of Rio
🚌 (2½ hrs) BR-101 as far as Rio Bonito, RJ 140 to Araruama, then RJ

106 as far as Búzios
🚌 (3 hrs) Cie 1001
📞 0800 25 10 01
● R$ 12.66

Petrópolis (4)

41 miles north of Rio
🚌 (1 hr) BR-040 (signs to Juiz de Fora) as far as Petrópolis
🚌 (1½ hrs) Cie Unica
☎ 263 87 92
● R$ 6

Teresópolis (5)

56 miles north of Rio
🚌 (1 hr 20 mins) BR 040 (Rio-Petrópolis) then BR 116 (signs to Teresópolis
🚌 (1½ hrs) Cie Teresópolis
☎ 233 46 25
● R$ 6.67

Vassouras (6)

72 miles northwest of Rio
🚌 (2 hrs) Take the Via Dutra (as far

as Barra Mensa), then the BR-393 (signs to Vassouras)
🚌 (2½ hrs) Cie Normandia
☎ 263 94 24
● R$ 9.75

Tiradentes (7)

199 miles north of Rio (Minas Gerais)
🚌 (4½ hrs) BR-040 as far as Barbacena, BR-265 as far as Tiradentes
🚌 Depart São João del Rei (20 mins) Cie Meier
☎ (032) 371 64 37
● R$ 1.30

São João del Rei (8)

208 miles north of Rio (Minas Gerais)
🚌 (4½ hrs) BR-040 (signs to Belo

Horizonte) as far as Barbacena, then BR-265 to São João del Rei
🚌 (5 hrs) Cie Paraibunas
☎ 253 08 94
● R$ 17.20 or 22.50 (luxury bus)

Belo Horizonte (9)

255 miles north of Rio (Minas Gerais)
🚌 (5½ hrs) BR-040 as far as Belo Horizonte
🚌 (6½ hrs) Cie Cometa
☎ 263 96 26
● R$ 21.67
By air (45 mins) from Santos

SERRA DA

Taubaté

1 Paraty

Jacareí

✈
BR116

SÃO PAULO

BR101

São Sebastião

São Vicente

4

2

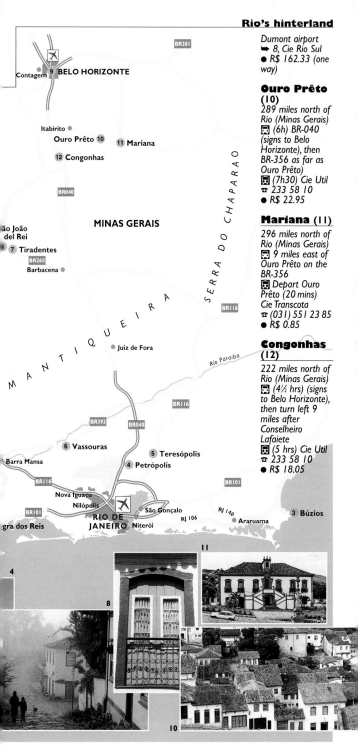

Rio's hinterland

Contagem 9 **BELO HORIZONTE**

BR381

Itabirito
Ouro Prêto 10   11 Mariana
12 Congonhas

BR040

MINAS GERAIS

ão João del Rei
8 7 Tiradentes
BR265
Barbacena

Juiz de Fora

Rio Paraíba

SERRA DO CHAPARÃO

M A N T I Q U E I R A

BR116
BR393   BR040

6 Vassouras
5 Teresópolis
Barra Mansa   4 Petrópolis

BR116
Nova Iguaçu
Nilópolis
BR101
gra dos Reis   **RIO DE JANEIRO**   Niterói   São Gonçalo
RJ 106   RJ 140   Araruama   3 Búzios
BR101

Dumont airport
➡ 8, Cie Rio Sul
● R$ 162.33 (one way)

Ouro Prêto (10)
289 miles north of Rio (Minas Gerais)
🚗 (6h) BR-040 (signs to Belo Horizonte), then BR-356 as far as Ouro Prêto)
🚌 (7h30) Cie Util
☎ 233 58 10
● R$ 22.95

Mariana (11)
296 miles north of Rio (Minas Gerais)
🚗 9 miles east of Ouro Prêto on the BR-356
🚌 Depart Ouro Prêto (20 mins) Cie Transcota
☎ (031) 551 23 85
● R$ 0.85

Congonhas (12)
222 miles north of Rio (Minas Gerais)
🚗 (4½ hrs) (signs to Belo Horizonte), then turn left 9 miles after Conselheiro Lafaiete
🚌 (5 hrs) Cie Util
☎ 233 58 10
● R$ 18.05

The 186 miles of coastline between Rio de Janeiro and Paraty is known as the Costa Verde because of its luxuriant tropical vegetation. There are many beaches, and little villages dating from the colonial era. To the northeast, the Costa do Sol extends as far as Cabo Frio and Arrial do Cabo, a region of white dunes and salt marshes, and on to Búzios. ■ Where to stay ➡ 26

 # Further afield

Paraty (1)

➡ 90 *Tourist information* ☎ *(024) 371 12 66*

Paraty (originally spelled Parati-y, from the name of a fish) is one of Brazil's most harmonious towns from an architectural point of view. It may lack the magnificence of the historic towns of the Minas Gerais, but this 18th-century port – which once handled cargoes of coffee and tobacco, then shipments of gold and silver – has remained intact. Original features include houses with thick walls, pitched roofs, colorful windows and carved wooden balconies, and streets paved in the *pé-de-moleque* (literally 'slave-foot') style. The most interesting buildings are the unfinished Matriz Nossa Senhora dos Remedios, the town's main place of worship, and the baroque church of Santa Rita. Built in 1722, beside the former prison, which is now a craft center, Santa Rita houses a museum of sacred art. There are no beaches at Paraty, but the islands in the bay can be reached by *saveiro* (a wooden boat typical of the Brazilian coast). They have magnificent beaches, where swimming is a real pleasure.

Angra dos Reis (2)

➡ 90 *Tourist information* ☎ *(024) 365 43 30*

The bay of Angra dos Reis is the only large bay in Brazil without a large city on its shores. It gives a sense of what Guanabara Bay must have been like a hundred years ago. Discovered on the day of Epiphany in the year 1502, it was named 'anchorage of the kings'. The bay is littered with almost 400 islands, including the superb Ilha Grande ➡ 26, Any stay at Angra dos Reis will include boat trips to admire the tropical vegetation. Little is left of the small town's colonial architecture, but do not miss the Convento São Bernardino de Sena. Although this is a tourist area, you should have no difficulty in finding a quiet, secluded inlet. The clear, warm waters of the bay are home to an amazing wealth of marine creatures.

Búzios (3)

➡ 90 *Tourist information* ☎ *(024) 623 20 99*

Búzios is said to have been discovered in the 16th century by Portuguese adventurers, who named it after a kind of shellfish (the whelk). But it was definitely the arrival of Brigitte Bardot in 1964 which made the place famous. On the two sides of the peninsula there are no less than 23 beaches. Frequented by the international jet-set, the resort has been compared to Ibiza or Saint-Tropez. It consists of three settlements: Manguingos, Armação and Praia dos Ossos (literally 'bone beach'). Praia is the most authentic, standing at the center of the peninsula, with its little Igreja Sant'Ana. The beaches in the immediate vicinity (Azeda, Azedhina and João Fernandes) are not surprisingly the most accessible and popular. They are easy to reach by road, or by boat if you take the Aquabus from Praia dos Ossos. The beaches of Ferradura (jet-ski hire) and Geribá (near Manguinhos, and favored by young people) can only be reached by car. At Armação, the hotels, good restaurants and smart boutiques are concentrated around the Rua das Pedras, which really comes to life between midnight and 4am.

Since the last century, the carioca bourgeoisie has been in the habit of migrating to the mountains in summer to escape Rio's torrid heat. From the impressive roads which climb up to the secluded resorts of Petrópolis and Teresópolis, there are wonderful views of the bay. Farther on, around Nova Friburgo, you can stop and enjoy the cool air and beautiful

Further afield

Petrópolis (4)

➡ 90 Tourist information 🆅 0800 24 1516

Petrópolis, 2,666 ft above sea level, was for many years Brazil's summer capital. On the orders of the emperor Dom Pedro II, the construction work was entrusted to Major Koeler. The twelve districts, laid out around squares, are defined by the three rivers on which the town is built. With its canals, the town is reminiscent of a European spa, and horse-drawn cabs ply for hire in the narrow paved streets of the central district. The Avenida Koeler, which follows the Quintandinha canal with its rows of venerable trees, leads to the strange residence of famous Brazilian pioneer aviator Santos Dumont, known as A Encantada. Depressed by the way aircraft were being used for military purposes, in 1918 Dumont retired to the spartan comforts of a house without furniture. Petrópolis still bears the stamp of Dom Pedro II. It is a simple, welcoming town, with some fine monuments in a skillfully managed natural setting. The Palácio Imperial, Dom Pedro's summer residence, was built in 1845 on the Fazenda do Córrego Seco, an estate purchased by his father. Slightly austere in its decoration, it now houses the Museu Imperial, and in particular the Brazilian crown jewels. Just outside Petrópolis, on the road to Rio, you cannot miss the hôtel-casino Quintandinha with its amazing Norman-style façade. The interior decoration is a Hollywoodian extravaganza. Opened in 1944, it was to be a casino, but soon afterward gambling was outlawed in Brazil. It is now a private club of fabulous luxury.

Teresópolis / Parque Nacional da Serra dos Orgãos (5)

➡ 90 Tourist information **Parque Nacional** ☎ (021) 642 10 70 🕒 Tue.–Sun. 8am–5pm ● entrance fee R$ 3; car R$ 5

Named in honor of the Empress Dona Teresa Cristina, wife of Dom Pedro II, Teresópolis stands 2,950 ft above sea level. Cooler even than Petrópolis, it is much favored by Cariocas as a summer resort. There are many interesting excursions in the immediate vicinity. The walk to Dedo de Deus mountain ('Finger of God', 5,550 ft) and the Serra dos Orgãos is undoubtedly the most spectacular. The mountains around here are extremely jagged, hence the name 'organ pipes'. The national park, established in 1939, is 25,000 acres in area. It consists of *floresta atlântica* (Atlantic-type virgin forest) with many rare species. Many visitors are attracted by the park's waterfalls, natural swimming pools and wild life.

Fazendas do Café (6)

➡ 90 Tourist information **Vassouras** ☎ (024) 471 12 90 **In Rio, Bon Voyage agency** ☎ 532 28 66

Rio de Janeiro state had many coffee plantations, the commodity on which the Brazilian economy was built in the 19th century. Beside the large area used for drying the coffee, stood the main residence and the *engenho*, where the coffee was cleaned. Apart from these features, the magnificent estates differ considerably in layout and design. Many are now private properties, closed to the public. This does not stop you take the Fazendas route from Santa Eufrasia to Santa Monica (near Vassouras).

surroundings at a *hotel-fazenda* (farm-hotel) in Murí, or at an inn in the charming town of Lumiar. ■ Where to stay ➥28

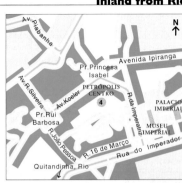

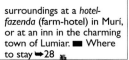

In 1789 the towns of the Minas Gerais were the scene of important historical events. Intrigued by the recent American revolution, teachers, lawyers and men of letters orchestrated a vain and tragic attempt to win independence from Portugal. It was known as the *Inconfidência Miniera* (the Minas conspiracy).

Further afield

Tiradentes (7)

➡ *90 Tourist information* ☎ *(032) 355 12 12*

Originally named Arrail da Ponta do Morro because it was built on a hill at the foot of the mountain, the town became Tiradentes in 1889, in honor of Joaquim da Silva Xavier, 'tooth puller' and heroic martyr of the *Inconfidência*. A colonial and mining town, Tiradentes still boasts period buildings, which hug the hillside. Its narrow paved streets are flanked by small houses with colorful windows and tiled roofs. Great efforts have been made to conserve the original buildings, thanks to Rodrigo Mello Franco de Andrade, founder of Brazil's historic and artistic heritage department. He began this task in 1928, taking up the concerns of 'modernist' architects and writers such as Mario de Andrade to establish a Brazilian national identity. Tiradentes has two main centers of interest: the central square, redesigned by Roberto Burle-Marx, and the Igreja da Matriz de Santo Antônio. Built in 1710, this is one of the most beautiful churches in Brazil. It is based on Portuguese models, but the abundance of gold in the decoration makes it more rococo than baroque, and it exhibits a certain clumsiness of proportion. It has two bell towers and a pediment by Aleijadinho. Another attractive feature of this very walkable town is the Chafirez de São José. Connected to the Mãe d'Água by an old stone aqueduct, this fountain, built in 1749, has three separate compartments: a public washtub, a horse trough, and a drinking-water basin. There is a small museum devoted to the Minas uprising.

São João del Rei (8)

➡ *90 Tourist information* ☎ *(032) 379 29 51*

Built on a small river, São João del Rei was one of the first towns born of Brazil's 18th-century gold rush. You can still travel to Tiradentes on the little steam railway dating from the beginning of the 20th century. The Victorian-style station has been converted into a railroad museum. Although São João is now a modern city, it has preserved its historic center and a wealth of old religious buildings. To get to the old part of town, you have to cross a particularly ugly modern district. Do not be put off! Begin your tour (preferably on foot) with the superb Igreja São Francisco de Assis (1774), whose attractive soapstone façade overlooks a square planted with imperial palms. Then walk down the Rua Padre José Maria Xavier to the Rosario bridge (1800). Cross the bridge and climb the steep street on your right (Rua Getúlio Vargas). This will bring you to the well-conserved precincts of the Igreja Nossa Senhora do Rosario (1708), the fine residence of the Tancredo Neves family (Brazil's first democratically elected president after the dictatorship), and the Igreja Nossa Senhora do Carmo. Return to your starting point by following the river (Avenida Presidente Tancredo Neves), from which you will be able to see the theater (1893) and the town hall (1849). São João del Rei is also famous for its pewterware. Pewter articles were used for everyday purposes in the 18th century. The technique was later revived by an Englishman, John Somers. In his former factory is a museum displaying some high-quality examples from the past.

Three hundred years ago, the Minas Gerais was the scene of the first gold rush in history. From 1715 to 1765, gold from the region was of world importance. When the veins were exhausted, Brazil's center of opportunity moved elsewhere, leaving the colonial architecture of most of these so-called 'historic' towns intact.

Further afield

Belo Horizonte (9)

➡ 90 Tourist information ☎ (031) 221 50 05 or (031) 220 13 10

Belo Horizonte, founded just a century ago (1897), is now Brazil's third largest city, population two million. Designed like a North-American city, the center is laid out to a grid plan. One of the city's most impressive features is the Pampulha district. Before becoming President of the Republic in 1956 and founder of Brasilia, Juscelino Kubitschek, for many years mayor of Belo Horizonte and governor of Minas state, commissioned Oscar Niemeyer to build this garden suburb around the lake (1940–2). The Igreja São Francisco de Assis, completed in 1943, is one of the most astonishing achievements of modern Brazilian architecture. It is constructed in a series of four waves, the largest being the nave. The chapel was decorated by Portinari, the exterior with *azulejos*, the interior with fresco paintings. The Pampulha development, all along the banks of the Lagoa, also includes water-sports clubs, a restaurant and dance hall, and a former casino, which is now the Museu de Arte de Pampulha. Belo Horizonte is a center of artistic creativity, in popular music (Uakti group), modern rhythms (Shank group), and dance (Grupo Corpo, which has an international reputation).

Ouro Prêto (10)

➡ 90 Tourist information ☎ (031) 559 32 69

In the 18th century the first nugget of gold was discovered here. With its paved streets, little houses with pantile roofs and sculpted fountains, Ouro Prêto has retained its old-world charm. In those days, with 80,000 inhabitants, the town was the wealthiest and most populous on the whole American continent, not excepting New York. Its most outstanding buildings are ecclesiastical. Those belonging to its early period, strongly influenced by European baroque, are the Matriz de Nossa Senhora de Conceição, built by Antônio Dias to plans by the father of Aleijadinho, the Capela do Padre Faria, and Nossa Senhora do Pilar. The second half of the 18th century was dominated by the work of Aleijadinho ('little cripple') himself. A half-caste, Antônio Francisco Lisboa (his real name, 1738–1814) produced sculptures of extraordinary expressive force (e.g. the Flagellation of Christ in the Museu da Inconfidência). He was also responsible for the façade of the Igreja Nossa Senhora do Carmo and his masterpiece, the Igreja São Francisco de Assis, thereby inaugurating a distinctive style: the *barroco mineiro*. The confraternity of the *Homens Pretos* (blacks) was not to be outdone and in 1762 commissioned Santa Ifigênia, a church which celebrates the story of Chico Rei, an African king transported to Brazil as a slave.

Not forgetting

■ **Mariana (11)** *Built around the important Catedral Basilica da Sé (designed by Aleijadinho's father), Mariana still has a good number of ecclesiastical and secular buildings from the time of its expansion as a mining town. Between Ouro Prêto and Mariana (5 miles from Ouro Prêto), it is possible to visit a former gold mine.* ➡ 90

■ **Congonhas (12)** *Here Aleijadinho carved the twelve prophets in soapstone, and seven scenes from Christ's Passion in polychrome wood.* ➡ 90

Map labels:
Ribeirão das Neves
Aeroporto de Confins
Município de Santa Luzia
Sta. Luzia
N
Av. Pedro I
LAOGOA DA PAMPULHA
MUSEU DE ARTE
Anel Rodoviário
IGREJA SÃO FRANCISCO DE ASSIS
Av. Cristiano Machado
Av. José C da Silveira
Sabará
Av. Atlântida
Av. A. Carlos
Av. D. Pedro II
Anel Rodoviário
Brasília
CENTRO
Av. dos Andradas
São Paulo
Av. Amazonas
Av. Raja Gabáglia
BELO HORIZONTE
9
Av. José P. Pontes
Nova Lima
Rio de Janeiro

Where to shop

Popular crafts

Two amazing boutiques, real museums of popular art.

Pé de Boi *Rua Ipiranga, 55 - Laranjeiras* ☎ 285 43 95
🕐 Mon.–Fri. 9am–7pm; Sat. 9am–1pm
Brumado *Rua das Laranjeiras, 486 - Laranjeiras* ☎ 558 22 75
🕐 Mon.–Fri. 9am–7pm; Sat. 10am–2pm

40
Stores

THE INSIDER'S FAVORITES

Local customs

Prices

As a reaction to the bad old days of galloping inflation, most of the articles on display do not have a price tag. The staff will be pleased to tell you what things cost.

Opening hours

Stores Mon.–Fri. 9am–7pm; Sat. 9am–1pm
Shopping malls Mon.–Sat. 9am–10pm; Sat. 9am–6.30pm
Some malls open on Sunday but in general it is only for their restaurants and play areas.

Shoes

As a general rule, you should ask for a size smaller than you normally wear.

Seasons

Note that, as Brazil is in the southern hemisphere, the seasons are out of step with those in Europe and North America: in December, store windows will be displaying the summer collections.

INDEX BY TYPE

The central district's first department store was built in the 1930s, following the French pattern. In the 1970s, American influence came to the fore with the creation of shopping centers. Here you will find most of the names normally associated with the retail trade, particularly in the fashion sector.

Where to shop

Rio Sul (1)
Avenida Lauro Müller, 116 - Botafogo ☎ 545 72 00

🅿 🕓 *Mon.–Sat. 10am–10pm; Sun 3–9pm* ▭

This major shopping center, conveniently situated between the beaches
➡ 80 and the Centro district, was the first of its kind in Rio. Now these big commercial centers are invading all the city's newly developed areas. A practical advantage of this one is that it is near the Canecão theater ➡ 54, so you can make a few purchases before the show, or have a snack. Take care not to get lost in its labyrinth of malls, escalators and 450 boutiques.

São Conrado Fashion Mall (2)
Estrada da Gávea, 899 - São Conrado ☎ 322 02 52

🕓 *Mon.–Thu. 10am–9pm; Fri.–Sat. 10am–11pm; Sun. 3–9pm* ▭
🏢 *Aqualund* ➡ *108, Lenny* ➡ *108, Valérie Le Heutre* ➡ *108, Frankie e Amaury*
➡ *108, Borogodó* ➡ *108*

With 146 shops and restaurants laid out on just two floors, this is the calmest, most sophisticated and most relaxing of Rio's shopping centers. It attracts a high-class clientele looking for quality rather than a wide range of merchandise. São Conrado beach ➡ 108 and the Gávea Golf Club ➡ 14 are just a short distance away.

Shopping Center da Gávea (3)
Rua Marquês de São Vicente, 52 - Gávea ☎ 294 10 96

🅿 🕓 *Mon.–Sat. 10am–10pm; Sun. noon–10pm (food shops and leisure activities)* ▭ 🏢 *John Sommers* ➡ *106, Enfim Enfant* ➡ *106, Andanças* ➡ *106, Gabriela* ➡ *106, Gramophone* ➡ *106*

Slightly outmoded, the Shopping Center da Gávea is nevertheless the commercial heart of this district. In the afternoons, it is thronging with children going to their dance or swimming lessons, which take place in the same complex. The mixed bag of 217 businesses includes antique dealers, interior decoration and furniture stores, jewelers, fashion boutiques, children's clothing and toy shops, art galleries and a Japanese restaurant.

Barrashopping (4)
Avenida das Américas, 4666 - Barra da Tijuca ☎ 431 99 22

🅿 🕓 *Mon.–Sat. 10am–10pm; Sun. 3–9pm* ▭ 🍴 🏢 *Aqualung* ➡ *108*

Barrashopping is a place in constant ferment. It has already been enlarged twice and is now Latin America's biggest shopping center. The complex houses 520 establishments, including restaurants of all kinds (pizza, sushis, salads), most of which are branches of downtown eating places. There is even an immense indoor fruit and vegetable market. The medical center upstairs is extremely modern and includes many specialists' practices.

Sta.
Tereza
Grajaú
Tijuca
Flamengo
JACAREPAGUÁ
Usina
PARQUE
NACIONAL
DA TIJUCA
Botafogo
PÃO DE
AÇÚCAR
1
Alto da
Boa Vista
Lagoa
3
LAGOA
DA TIJUCA
Itanhangá
Copacabana
4
São
Conrado
Ipanema
Barra
da Tijuca
Joá
2
Oceano Atlântico
N

1

4

4

3

2

In the area

The Rua Visconde de Pirajá and the streets between it and the beach are Rio's traditional chic shopping area. Especially pleasant are the boutiques in Rua Aníbal de Mendonça, where you can stroll under shady trees.
■ Where to stay ➥ 22 ■ Where to eat ➥ 34 ➥ 36

➡ Where to shop

Garapa Doida (5)
Rua Carlos Góis, 234 (Loja F) - Leblon ☎ 274 81 86 ➥ 274 81 86

Spirits 🅿 🕐 *Mon. 4–8pm; Tue.–Fri. 11am–8pm; Sat. 11am–6pm* ▢

Tucked away in a quiet Leblon street, this little boutique is a paradise for lovers of *cachaça* (an alcoholic drink made from sugar cane). Young or aged in the barrel, drunk neat or mixed with coconut milk or fruit juice to make a *batida*, or poured on lime and crushed ice as a *caipirinha*, every *cachaça* has its moment. ★ Try one in the shop.

H. Stern (6)
Rua Visconde de Pirajá, 490 - Ipanema ☎ 274 34 47

Jewelry 🕐 *Mon.–Fri. 10am–7.30pm; Sat. 10am–2pm* ▢ 🔀 *Avenida Rio Branco, 177 ☎ 220 19 36 ; Copacabana Palace ☎ 235 31 37*

Tourmalines in a range of hues, aquamarines, amethysts, topaz and opals, not to mention rubies, emeralds, sapphires and diamonds: precious stones are one of Brazil's enduring attractions. The H. Stern shops display them with panache, offering an incomparable choice of styles and prices. ★ Visit the workshop on the 3rd floor where you can see the gems being weighed and gold being fashioned.

Francesca Romana (7)
Rua Visconde de Pirajá, 351 (1st floor) - Ipanema ☎ 521 08 77

Jewelry 🕐 *Mon.–Fri. 10am–7pm; Sat. 10am–2pm* ▢

Francesca Romana's necklaces, earrings and rings combine the sophistication of Italian design with the colorful diversity of Brazil's precious stones. You will be captivated by her large agate or onyx signet rings set with a sparkling cabochon.

Letras & Expressões (8)
Rua Visconde de Pirajá, 276 - Ipanema ☎ 521 61 10

Books, newspapers 🕐 *Mon.–Thu. 8am–2am; Fri.–Sun. 24 hours* ▢

Latest of this chain of 'super-news-stands', the Ipanema branch extends to two floors, stocking a vast range of foreign and Brazilian magazines and newspapers, as well as some CDs and smokers' necessities. You are bound to find *The Daily Telegraph, The Times* or *The New York Times*.

Not forgetting

■ **Glorinha Paranaguá (9)** Rua Visconde de Pirajá, 365-B (Loja 2) - Ipanema ☎ 522 82 03 *Charming little handbags for evening wear or smart lunch parties.* ■ **Superpasso (10)** Rua Conde de Bernadotte, 26 - Leblon ☎ 512 80 89 *On Thursdays and Saturdays, this store receives deliveries of oddments and prototypes of shoes and sandals made for export. Unbeatable prices.* ■ **Salinas (11)** Rua Visconde de Pirajá, 547 (Loja 211) - Ipanema ☎ 274 06 44 *Bright, flowery bathing costumes for girls and young women.* ■ **Collector's (12)** Rua Visconde de Pirajá, 550 (Loja 110)- Ipanema ☎ 239 67 93 ➥ 239 63 67 *This is the place to unearth rare Brazilian music from the 1930s, 1940s and 1950s. The shop stocks CDs, LPs and even old 78s!*

- After dark ➡ 50
- ➡ 52 ➡ 54
- What to see ➡ 80

Ipanema's Rua Visconde de Pirajá, the in-place to shop for fashion wear and smart jewelry.

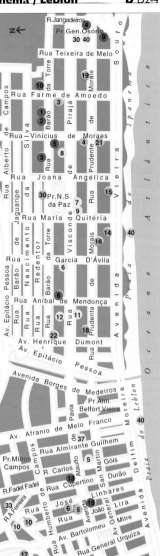

In the area

Not far from the Jardim Botânico and the racecourse, the mainly residential Gávea district is of no special interest to the tourist. However, the Shopping Center da Gávea has a good range of boutiques of various kinds, and theaters.

Where to shop

John Somers (13)

Shopping Center da Gávea ➡ 102
Rua Marquês de São Vicente, 52 (Loja 305) - Gávea ☎ 512 87 80

Interior decoration, pewterware ⊙ *Mon.–Fri. 10am–9pm; Sat. 10am–8pm* ▭

Manufactured and hand-finished at São João del Rei (Minas Gerais) ➡ 96 in the finest tradition of 17th- and 18th-century craftsmanship, John Somers pewterware ranges from unremarkable ashtrays to stunning chandeliers. There is a very good selection of tableware, and the tea and coffee services, with jacaranda wood handles, are justly famous. The highly original Utrecht line consists of reproductions of items (spoons, condiment sets, pitchers) salvaged in 1981 from the wreck of a Dutch frigate of that name which was sunk in 1648 during an engagement with the Portuguese off Itaparica (Bahia).

Enfim Enfant (14)

Shopping Center da Gávea ➡ 102
Rua Marquês de São Vicente, 52 (Loja 353) - Gávea ☎ 239 92 98

Toys 🅿 ⊙ *Mon.–Sat. 10am–9pm* ▭

Papier-mâché puppets, puppet theaters, rag dolls, puzzles of all kinds and giant dominos: Enfim Enfant is an Aladdin's cave of unusual or forgotten toys, intelligent, curious, educational and creative. Girls will probably adore the wooden dolls' houses with their miniature furniture, while boys will make a beeline for the lead soldiers.

Andanças (15)

Shopping Center da Gávea ➡ 102
Rua Marquês de São Vicente, 52 (Loja 324) - Gávea ☎ 239 30 48

Crafts 🅿 ⊙ *Mon.–Fri. 10am–9pm; Sat. 10am–8pm* ▭

The items of popular art displayed here come from various parts of Brazil. Take a good look at the little painted figurines from Penambucco of chessmen and people doing different jobs, and do not miss the maçaranduba-wood animals from the Minas Gerais (lions, parrots, monkeys). The stool in the form of a stylized toad is alone worth the visit, provided you have no problems with excess baggage! The collections of lead-painted fruits and African heads are also fascinating. The prices are affordable, and you can be sure of a warm welcome.

Not forgetting

■ **Bookmakers (16)** Rua Marquês de São Vicente, 7 - Gávea
☎ 239 24 45 *This little friendly store stocks books in several languages and is much in demand with artists and poets wishing to launch their works.*
■ **Gramophone (17)** Shopping Center da Gávea, Rua Marquês de São Vicente, 52 (Loja 107) - Gávea ☎ 274 24 95 *The strength of this record store is MPB (música popular brasileira). You will find all the stars of bossa-nova, at modest prices. Why not get the complete works? The service is excellent.*

■ Where to eat ➡ 38
■ After dark ➡ 52 ➡ 54
➡ 56 ■ What to see ➡ 82

John Somers old-style pewterware is a reminder of the short-lived luxury of gold-rush times.

Through the Dois Irmãos tunnel, the fine buildings of the São Conrado district stand facing the sea, in striking contrast with the favela of Rocinha. Open to the sky and planted with lush vegetation, the Fashion Mall ➡ 102 is one of the most elegant places to shop in Rio.

Where to shop

Aqualung (18)
Barrashopping ➡ 102
Av. das Americas, 4666 (Parte 22, Loja 106) - Barra da Tijuca

Sportswear 🅿 🕐 *Mon.–Sat. 10am–10pm* ▭ 🔌 *Rua Visconde de Pirajá, 444 (Loja 121)*

The Aqualung ecological institute helps fund a number of projects to conserve Brazilian wildlife, particularly threatened marine species such as whales and turtles. As part of the fund-raising, they sell some superb T-shirts with marine motifs. The Aqualung style, featuring creative designs and pastel colors, is highly distinctive. Sizes for two-year-olds upward. The company also markets a sportswear range.

Lenny (19)
São Conrado Fashion Mall ➡ 102
Estrada da Gávea, 899 (Loja 217) - São Conrado ☎ 322 25 61

Swimming costumes 🅿 🕐 *Mon.–Thu. 10am–10pm; Fri.–Sat. 10am–11pm* ▭ 🔌 *Shopping Rio Sul ➡ 102; Rua Visconde de Pirajá, 351 (Loja 224)*

Bikinis and one-piece costumes, print and plain fabrics, at Lenny's the accent is very much on sophistication and elegance. These women's costumes can be worn with a shirt, shorts or a matching *paréo*.
NB: there is a wider choice between November and February (summer collection). Some models are available in girls' sizes, in the same fabrics as the adult costumes. The company also has a branch at Búzios ➡ 92.

Valérie Le Heutre (20)
São Conrado Fashion Mall ➡ 102
Estrada da Gávea, 899 (Loja 109-A) - São Conrado ☎ 322 47 44

Jewelry 🅿 🕐 *Mon.–Sat. 10am–10pm* ▭

With names such as 'La Vie en rose', 'Matelassé', 'Spring' and 'New York', it must be said that the jewelry collections designed by Valérie Le Heutre have character. This French designer has settled in Rio, where she sells exclusive jewelry, sometimes featuring gems of unusual color. Let yourself be tempted by the shapes and textures of her rings, each of which is a highly individual creation. Sheer luxury!

Not forgetting

■ **Legep (21)** Avenida das Américas, Recreio dos Bandeirantes, 16551 - Barra da Tijuca ☎ 437 89 57 ➡ 437 86 41 *Huge stock of unworked Brazilian semiprecious stones, used for interior decoration* ■ **Frankie e Amaury (22)** Fashion Mall ➡ 102, Estrada da Gávea, 899 (Loja 214-D) - Gávea ☎ 322 12 25 *Ready-to-wear women's clothing and accessories in leather and suede. The trompe-l'oeil decoration is worth a visit for its own sake.*
■ **Borogodó (23)** Fashion Mall ➡ 102, Estrada da Gávea, 899 (Loja 114-A) - Gávea ☎ 322 19 37 *An unprepossessing boutique, but full of good things. Hand-embroidered sheets and tablecloths in linen and percale.*

You will find many original items in Rio's shops, not least at the São Conrado Fashion Mall.

In the area

The Centro is quite unlike the rest of Rio. No time for a leisurely stroll, you have to go with the flow. The Saara district is a hive of commercial activity, where you shop to the sound of canned music. ■ Where to stay ➡ 24 ■ Where to eat ➡ 46 ■ After dark ➡ 52 ➡ 56 ■ What to see

Where to shop

Saraiva Megastore (24)
Rua do Ouvidor, 98 - Centro ☎ 507 95 00 ➡ 509 16 20

Ⓜ Carioca **Books, newspapers** 🕐 Mon.–Fri. 8.30am–7.30pm; Sat. 8.30am–1.30pm ▭

With 15,000 square feet of floor space, the Saraiva Megastore stocks some 90,000 different articles: books, periodicals, multimedia products, stationery, CDs and videos. There are optical scanner terminals to tell you the prices. The Saraiva Music Hall, on the first floor, is devoted to music in all its forms, with an effective search facility, 38 audio booths and an area reserved for jazz and classical music.

Livraria Leonardo Da Vinci (25)
Avenida Rio Branco, 185 (Lojas 2, 3, 9) - Centro ☎ 533 22 37

Ⓜ Carioca **Books, newspapers** 🕐 Mon.–Fri. 9am–7pm; Sat. 9am–12.30pm ▭

This very traditional bookstore is located in the basement of an office building, down an amazingly convoluted staircase. On its crowded shelves, you will find the best selection of foreign books in Rio. The company will order you books from other countries.

Casa Turuna (26)
Rua Senhor dos Passos, 122-124 - Saara ☎ 509 39 08 ➡ 242 91 87

Ⓜ Uruguaiana **Fancy dress** 🕐 Mon.–Fri. 9am–6.30pm; Sat. 8.30am–1pm ▭

This business, founded in 1915, sells everything you could possibly need for making your carnival costume: feathers, spangles and paste jewelry in profusion. And why not take home one of their papier-mâché animal-head masks?

Maximino (27)
Avenida Rio Branco, 25 - Centro ☎ 233 53 84 ➡ 253 24 75

Ⓜ Uruguaiana **Gemstones** 🕐 Mon.–Fri. 9am–6pm ▭

You can expect a friendly welcome in this store, whose somewhat dated fittings confirm that Maximino's has seen a steady stream of tourists over the years. Get them to bring you a batch of cut stones in the size and color you are looking for, and take time making your selection.
★ One piece of advice: the khaki, green and brown décor is far from ideal when it comes to appreciating the color of the stones. Insist on examining them near the window, in daylight. You can buy loose stones and some finished pieces of jewelry.

Not forgetting

■ **Casa Azevedo (28)** Rua Senhor dos Passos, 63 - Saara ☎ 242 11 09
Sequins by the yard, imitation gems, buttons and glass beads, polished stones for making up into necklaces: this drugstore is a mine of showy stuff. More interesting are the local shells of different sizes, with their delicate mother-of-pearl interiors.
■ **J. Asmar e Cia. (29)** Rua Senhor dos Passos, 233 - Saara
☎ 224 02 78 *Pará and cashew nuts, dried fruit and spices.*

➡ 68
➡ 70 ➡ 72
➡ 78

26

27

29

Feiras are the open-air food markets around which the lives of Rio families revolve. Each district has its *feira day*, a riot of color, with customers crowding round the busy stands from 7am. Antiques dealers and sellers of secondhand goods normally do business on Saturdays and Sundays at *feiras de antigüidades*. Some of these markets take place in the

➡ **Shopping**

COBAL LEBLO
ESTACIONAMENTO
24h ROTAT
PERN
MEN

Feira de Ipanema (30)

Praça General Osório - Ipanema
Foodstuffs
🕐 Tue. 7am–1pm

An abundance of excellent produce for sale, behind the very chic Avenida Vieira Souto.

Rui Barbosa (31)

Praça Nicarágua, Osvaldo Cruz corner
Ⓜ Flamengo
Foodstuffs
🕐 Wed. 7am–noon
In a magnificent setting, overlooked by the Corcovado ➡ 84, with views of the Pão de Açúcar.

Feira de Glória (32)

Rua Augusto Severo
Ⓜ Glória
Foodstuffs
🕐 Sun. 7am–noon
Another atmospheric place in which to stock up on fruit and vegetables.

Cobal Leblon (33)

Rua Gilberto Cardoso - Leblon
☎ 239 15 49
Foodstuffs
🕐 Tue.–Sat. 8am–6pm; Sun. 8am–1pm
Indoor market selling fruit, vegetables, meat, fish, spices, flowers, cheese, confectionery, etc. The Cobal and its improvised cafés

are a feature of the Leblon district. On Saturdays, writers, journalists and popular singers can be seen here, taking an aperitif.

Praça XV de Novembro (34)

Praça XV de Novembro - Centro
Ⓜ Carioca
Secondhand goods, antiques
🕐 Sat. 9am–1pm
Two markets liven up this area: the antiques market has some rare items (but they're not cheap). Good deals can be found just next door at the Feira 'Troco'.

Praça Santos Dumont (35)

Praça Santos Dumont - Gávea
Antiques, secondhand goods
🕐 Sun. 9am–4pm
A fairly small market, with some unusual items on sale. Rather kitsch.

Rua do Lavradio (36)

Rua do Lavradio - Centro
Ⓜ Carioca
Secondhand goods, antiques
🕐 1st Sat. of the month
On that Saturday the street is cleared of traffic

open air; others have migrated to indoor shopping centers.

Markets and antiques fairs

and the second-hand dealers who sell from their stores during the week spill out into the roadway. Some items more genuine than others.

Rio Design Center (37)

Avenida Ataulfo de Paiva, 270 - Leblon
☎ 540 07 00
Secondhand goods, antiques
P

☒ *Sun. 11am–7pm.*
From Monday to Saturday, the boutiques in the Rio Design Center sell contemporary furniture and decorative items.

On Sundays, the walkways are crowded with stalls selling silverware, crockery, knick-knacks and old jewelry. ★ Do not hesitate to bargain: prices tend to be somewhat inflated.

Shopping Cassino Atlântico (38)

Avenida Atlântica, 4240 - Copacabana
☎ 523 87 09
Secondhand goods, antiques
☒ *Mon.–Fri. 9am–9pm; Sat. 9am–8pm*

This arcade houses antiques dealers. On Saturdays, some of them stay open to take part in the market, and other dealers set up stalls in the walkways.
★ Good selection of antique jewelry in the basement.

Rua Siqueira Campos, 143 (39)

Rua Siqueira Campos, 143 - Copacabana
Secondhand goods, antiques
☒ *Mon.– Fri. 10am–6pm; Sat. 10am–1pm*
This is Rio's other

main antiques center, on a par with the Cassino Atlântico arcade.

Feira Hippie (40)

Praça General Osório - Ipanema
Popular art, crafts
☒ *Sun. 9am–6pm*
The famous Feira Hippie, a magnet for tourists, offers a vast range of craft products. There is a good selection of naive paintings in different styles, at affordable prices. The Feira also has a number of jewelry and leather-goods stands.

The 'zonas' of Rio de Janeiro

Rio is made up of four main *zonas* (zones): *zona norte* (north), *zona sul* (south), *zona oeste* (west), and *centro* (the city center). Each zone subdivides into a number of districts. The north and west zones are industrial in character, and a long way from the beaches.

Finding your way

Centro

This is the business district and the throbbing heart of the city, feverishly busy in the daytime. It is bounded by the bay on one side, and by the south and north zones on the other. It is deserted at night, except for one or two hot-spots.

Zona sul

This is the wealthy side of town, with the best shops and restaurants, the most prestigious residential areas, the beaches, and such well-known districts as Ipanema and Copacabana.

7
Maps

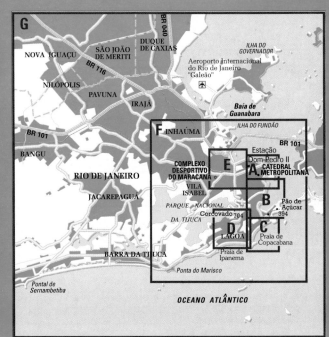

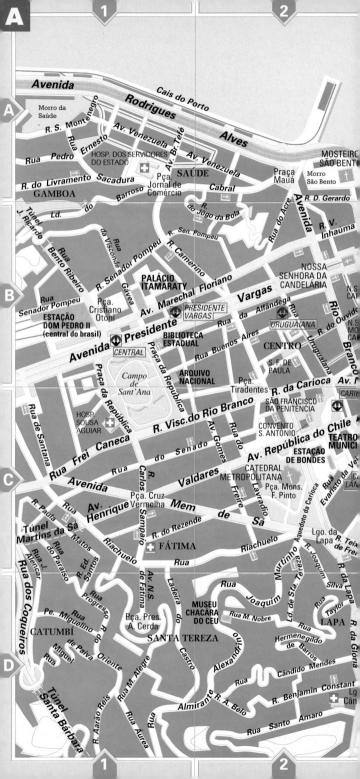

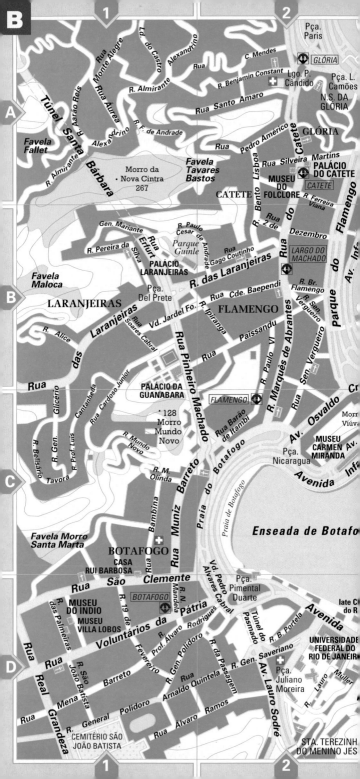

OCEANO ATLÂNTICO

Baía de Guanabara

MARINA
A GLORIA

Flamengo
do Flamengo

Henriq

Fortaleza
De São João

. 72
Morro
Cara de Cão

Alves

João Luís

Av.

R. Cândido Gaffrée

Alameda Flóriano

URCA

Portugal

R. Marechal Cantuária

. Pão de Açúcar
394

250

Morro da Urca
218

Avenida

Rua R. Franco

E. de
eira

Pasteur

Pça.
General
Tiburcio

Praia
Vermelha

a
in
nt

ESTAÇÃO PARA
O PÃO DE AÇÚCAR

Morro
da Babilônia
235

1:23000

0   250   500 m

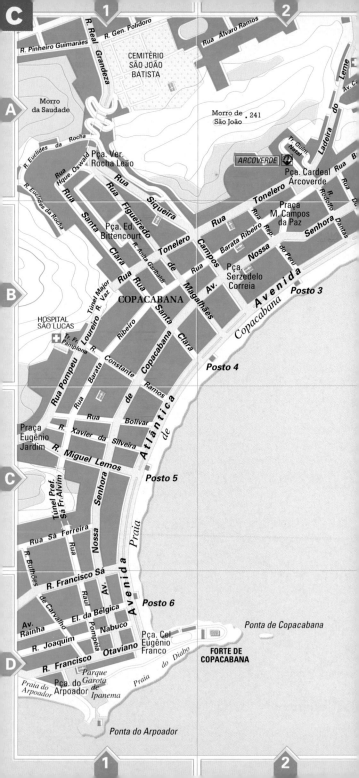

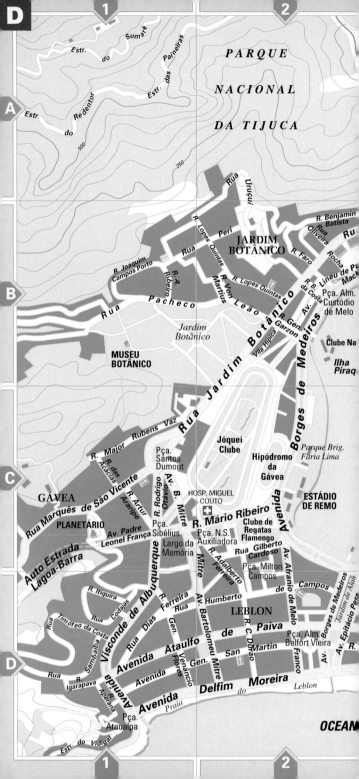

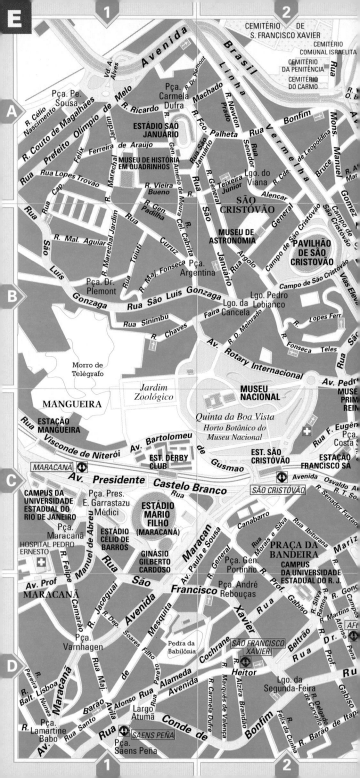

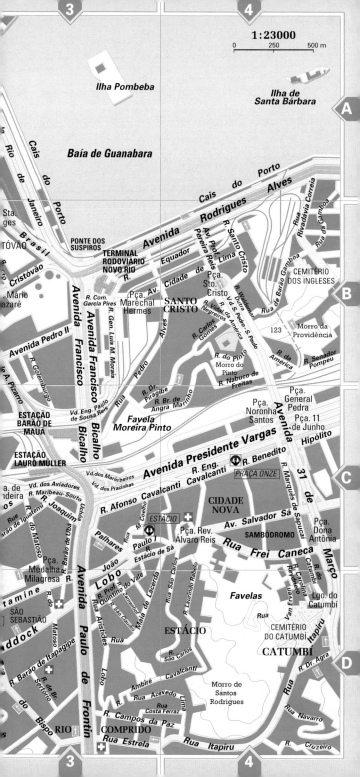

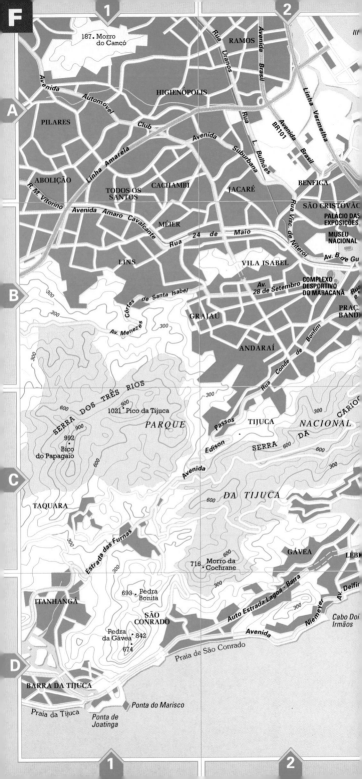

G

1 **2**

BELFORD ROXO

Canal Sarapui

DUQUE

Rodovia

SÃO JOÃO
DE MERITI

NOVA IGUAÇU

Presidente

A

Dutra

Rio São João

Can. da Pavuna

500 300 100

Rio Sarapui

BR116

NILÓPOLIS

PAVUNA

ANCHIETA

IRAJÁ

Rio da Pavuna

BR101

Avenida

Avenida Brasil

MADUREIRA

Automóv

B

BANGU

R

100 100 100 300

500
300
700 300

954 • Morro
da Bandeira

100

300

500

1022 • Pedra
Branca

SERRA DO QUILOMBO

724 300

300

JACAREPAGUÁ

500

500

758 • Pedra do
Quilombo

300 100

Rio do Abril

300

714 • Pico do
Sacarrão

500

C

500

300

100

AUTÓDROMO DO
RIO DE JANEIRO

100

Avenida Salvador Allende

Lagoa de
Jacarepaguá

AEROPORTO
DE JACAREPAGUA

Lagoa
da Tijuca

100

Canal do Cortado

das

Américas

BARRA DA TIJUC

Avenida

Lagoa
de Marapendi

Sernambetiba

Praia Barra da Tijuca

Avenida

RECREIOS DOS
BANDEIRANTES

I. da
Alfavaca

Pontal de
Sernambetiba

I. Pontuda

D

OCEANO

1 **2**

CAXIAS

Ilha do
Boqueirão

Ilha de
Paquetá

A

AEROPORTO INTERNACIONAL
DO RIO DE JANEIRO
"GALEÃO-ANTÔNIO CARLOS JOBIM"

Linha Vermelha

Avenida Brasil

NHA

I. d'Água

Ilha do
Governador

I. do Engenho

RAMOS

Ilha do Fundão

IAÚMA

B a í a

arela Clube

Ponte de Niterói

BR101

B

SÃO
CRISTÓVÃO

Cais do Porto

d e

ER

ESTAÇÃO
DOM PEDRO II

G u a n a b a r a

JANEIRO

CENTRO

NITERÓI

RIO COMPRIDO

AEROPORTO
"SANTOS DUMONT"

VILA
ISABEL

500

FLAMENGO

100

CARIOCA

RQUE

NACIONÁL

DA

Corcovado
• 704

394 • Pão de
Açúcar

SERRA

300

BOTAFOGO

300

DA TIJUCA

I. Cotunduba

C

500

COPACABANA

GÁVEA

LAGOA

Praia
de Copacabana

300

LEBLON

IPANEMA

500

100

Ponta de
Copacabana

SÃO
NRADO

Praia de Ipanema

Praia
São Conrado

Ponta do
Marisco

I. das Palmas

I. Cagarra

• I. do Mejo

I. Comprida

D

A T L Â N T I C O

Ilha Rasa

I. Redonda

1 : 200 000

0   2   4 km

3

4

Street index

Each street name is followed by a bold letter indicating which map to refer to, and a grid reference.

Index

Botafogo (Metrô)
B D I
Botânico *Jardim-*
D B I-2
Branca *Pedra-* **G** C I
Branco Castelo
Presidente *Avenida-*
E C I-2
Brazil *Avenida-*
G A-B I-3
Bruce General *Rua-*
E A-B 2
Buenos Aires *Rua-*
A B 2
Bulhões de Carvalho
Rua- **C** C-D I

C

Cabríta Coronel *Rua-*
E B I
Cabritos *Morro dos-*
D B 4
Cachambi **F** A I
Cagarra *Ilha-* **G** D 4
Caiçaras *Ilha dos-*
D C 3
Câmara Cardeal
Praça- **A** C 2
Câmara Marechal
Avenida- **A** C 3
Camerino *Rua-*
A B I-2
Campo de Santana
A B-C I
Campos da Paz *Rua-*
E D 3-4
Campos da Paz
Manuel *Praça da-*
C B 2
Campus da Escola
Naval **A** C 4
Campus da
Universidade
Estadual do Rio
de Janeiro **E** C-D 2
Campus da
Universidade
Estadual do Rio
de Janeiro **E** C I
Canabarro General
Rua- **E** C-D 2
Cancela *Largo da-*
E B 2
Cancó *Morro do-*
F A I
Cândido Gaffrée *Rua-*
B C 3-4
Cândido Mendes
Rua- **A** D 2
Cantagalo *Morro do-*
D C 4
Cantagalo *Parque do-*
D C 4
Cantuária Marechal
Rua- **B** C-D 3
Cap. Félix *Rua-*
E A-B I
Cara de Cão *Morro-*
B C 4
Cardoso Júnior *Rua-*
B B-C I
Carioca **A** C 2
Carioca *Aqueduto da-*
A C 2
Carioca *Rua da-*
A B-C 2
Carioca *Serra da-*
G C 3

Carlos Peixoto
Avenida- **C** A 2-3
Carlos Sempaio *Rua-*
A C I
Carmela Dufre *Praça-*
E A I
Carmela Dufre *Rua-*
E D 2
Carmen Miranda
Museu- **B** C 2
Carmo *Cemitério do-*
E A 2
Carolina Reydnero
Rua- **E** C-D 4
Carpológico *Museu-*
D C I
Casa Rui Barbosa
B C I
Castelo **A** C 3
Castro *Ladeira do-*
A D I
Catedral
Metropolitana **F** B 3
Catete **B** A 2
Catete *Palácio do-*
B A 2
Catete *Rua do-*
B A-B 2
Catete (Metrô) **B** A 2
Catumbí **A** D I
Catumbí *Cemitério
do-* **E** D 4
Catumbí *Largo do-*
E D 4
Catumbí *Rua do-*
E C-D 4
Cavalcanti
Engenheiro *Rua-*
E C 4
Caxias Duque de
Forte- **C** A 4
Ceara *Rua-* **E** C 2
Celio de Barros
Estádio- **E** C I
Célio Nascimento
Rua- **E** A I
Cemetério São João
Batista **B** D I
Cemitério Comunal
Israelita **E** A 2
Cemitério
da Penitência **E** A 2
Cemitério de São
Francisco Xavier
E A 2
Cemitério do Carmo
E A 2
Cemitério do
Catumbí **E** D 4
Cemitério dos
Ingleses **E** B 4
Central *Estação-*
A C 4
Central (Metrô)
A B I
Cesário Alvini *Rua-*
D A 4
Chafariz das
Saracuras **D** D 4
Charara do Ceu
Museu- **A** D I-2
Chaves Faira *Rua-*
E B I-2
Churchill *Avenida-*
A C 3
Cidade de Lima
Avenida- **E** B 3-4
Cidade Nova **E** C 4
Cinelândia **A** C 2

Clube de Regatas
Flamengo **D** C 2
Clube Naval **D** B 2
Cobras *Ilha das-*
F A 3-4
Cochrane *Morro da-*
F C 2
Codajás *Rua-* **D** D I
Coelho Cintra
Engenheiro *Túnel-*
C A 2-3
Coelho Machado
Rua- **E** C 3
Complexo Esportivo
do Maracanã **F** B 2
Comprida *Ilha-*
G D 3-4
Comunal Israelita
Cemitério- **E** A 2
Conceição *Morro da-*
A B 2
Convento São
Antônio **A** C 2
Copacabana **G** C 3-4
Copacabana
Ponta de- **G** C 4
Copacabana *Praia de-*
G C 4
Coqueiros *Rua dos-*
A C-D I
Corcovado **G** C 3
Cortado *Canal do-*
G C I
Cosme Velho **F** C 3
Cotunduba *Ilha-*
G C 4
Coutinho Gago *Rua-*
B B 2
Cristiano Otoni
Praça- **A** B I
Cristo Redentor
F C 3
Cruzeiro *Rua-* **E** D 4
Cupertino Durão
Rua- **D** D 2
Curuzu *Rua-* **E** B I
Custódio de Melo
Almirante *Praça-*
D B 2

D

Da Costa e Silva
Ponte *Pres.A.-* **G** B 4
Delfim Moreira
Avenida- **D** D I-2
Delgado de Carlallo
Rua- **E** D 2
Del Prete *Praça-*
B B I
Deputado Soares
Filho *Rua-* **E** D I
Derby Club *Estação-*
E C I
Dezenove de
Fevereiro *Rua-*
B D I
Diabo *Praia do-*
C D I
Dois Irmãos *Cabo-*
F D 2
Doze de Dezembro
Rua- **B** B 2
Duarte Pimental
Praça- **B** D 2
Duque de Caxias
G A 2-3
Dutra Presidente
Rodovia- **G** A I-2

Duvivier *Rua-*
C A-B 2

E

Edison Passos
Avenida- **F** C I-2
Edmundo Bittencourt
Praça- **C** B I
Elizabeth Rainha
Avenida- **C** D I
Emílio Garrastazu
Presidente *Praça-*
E C I
Engenho *Ilha do-*
G A 4
Enxadas *Ilha da-*
F A 3-4
Episcopal *Palácio-*
A B 2
Equador *Rua-*
E B 3-4
Erfurt *Rua-* **B** B I
Escobar *Rua-* **E** B 2
Escola da Artes
Visuais do Parque
Lage **D** A 3
Escola Naval
Campus da- **A** C 4
Escultura *Bosque-*
B A 3
Estação Barão
de Mauá **E** C 3
Estação de Bondes
A C 2
Estação Derby Club
E C I
Estação Dom
Pedro II **F** B 3
Estação Francisco Sá
E C 2
Estação Lauro Müller
E C 3
Estação Mangueira
E C I
Estação Parao Pão
de Açucar **B** D 3
Estação São
Cristóvão **E** C 2
Estácio **E** D 4
Estácio (Metrô)
E C 3-4
Estácio de Sá *Rua-*
E C 3-4
Estádio Celio de
Barros **E** C I
Estádio de Remo
D C 2
Estádio Mario Filho
(Maracanã) **E** C I
Estádio Vasco
da Gama **E** A I
Estadual *Biblioteca-*
A B I-2
Estadual do Rio
de Janeiro *Campus
da Universidade-*
A B-C I
Estrela *Rua-* **E** D 3
Estudantes
Travessa dos- **A** C 3
Euclides da Rocha
Rua- **C** A-B I
Eugênio Jardim *Praça-*
C C I
Eugênuo Franco
Coronel *Praça-* **C** D I
Euzébio Oliveira
Praça- **B** D 3

P

Paço Imperial **A** B 3
Padilha General *Rua-*
E A-B I
Paissandu *Rua-*
B B 2
Palácio da Guanabara
B B-C I
Palácio do Catete
B A 2
Palácio Itamaraty
A B I
Palácio Laranjeiras
B B I
Palmas *Ilha das-*
G D 3
Palmeiras *Rua das-*
B D I
Papagaio *Bico do-*
F C I
Paquetá *Ilha de-* **G** A 4
Paraíso *Rua do-*
A C-D I
Para o Pão de Açucar
Estação- **B** D 3
Pareto *Rua-* **E** D I
Paris *Praça-* **B** A 2
Parque Brigadeiro
Faria Lima **D** C 2
Parque do Cantagalo
D C 4
Parque do Flamengo
B A-B 2-3
Parque Garota
de Ipanema **C** D I
Parque General
Leandro **B** D 2
Parque Guinle **B** B I
Parque Lage **D** B 3
Parque Nacional
da Tijuca **G** C I
Parque Vila Formosa
E B 4
Pasmado *Túnel do-*
B D 2
Passagem *Rua da-*
B D 2
Pasteur *Avenida-*
B D 2-3
Paul Claudel *Praça-*
D D 2-3
Paula Cândido *Largo-*
A D 2-3
Paula e Sousa
Avenida- **E** C-D I-2
Paula Matos *Rua-*
A C I
Paulo de Frontin
Avenida- **F** B 3
Paulo de Sousa Reis
Engenheiro *Viaduto-*
E C 3
Paulo I João *Rua-*
E C-D 3
Paulo VI *Rua-* **B** B 2
Pavao *Morro da-*
D D 4
Pavuna **G** A 2
Pavuna *Canal da-*
G A 2
Pavuna *Rio da-*
G A-B I
Pedra General *Praça-*
E C 4
Pedro Alvares Cabral
Viaduto- **B** C-D 2
Pedro Alves *Rua-*
E B-C 3-4
Pedro Américo *Rua-*

B A 2
Pedro Ernesto
Hospital- **E** C I
Pedro Ernesto *Rua-*
E B 4
Pedro II *Avenida-*
E B 2
Pedro II *Praça-* **E** B 2
Pedro II Dom
Estação- **F** B 3
Pedro Lobianco
Largo- **E** B 2
Penha **G** A 3
Penitência
Cemitério da- **E** A 2
Pereira da Silva *Rua-*
B B I
Pereira M. *Rua-*
D A 4
Pereira Nunes *Rua-*
E D I
Pereira Reis Professor
Avenida- **E** B 4
Peri *Rua-* **D** B 2
Pessoa Epitácio
Avenida- **D** B-D 2-3
Pilares **F** A I
Pinto *Morro do-* **E** B 4
Pinto *Rua do-* **E** B 4
Pio X *Praça-* **A** B 2
Piragibe Doutor *Rua-*
E C 3-4
Pirajá Visconde de
Rua- **D** D 3-4
Piraquê *Ilha-* **D** B 2
Pistóia *Praça-* **A** D 3
Planetário **D** C I
Plemont Doutor
Praça- **E** B I
Plemont Doutor *Rua-*
E A I-2
Polidoro General
Rua- **B** D I
Pombeba *Ilha-* **F** A 3
Pompeu Loureiro
Rua- **D** C 4
Pompeu Senador
Rua- **A** B I-2
Ponte de Niterói
F A 3-4
Pontuda *Ilha-* **G** D 2
Portinho General
Praça- **E** C 2
Porto *Cais do-*
G B 3-4
Portugal *Avenida-*
B C-D 3
Praça da Bandeira
F B 2-3
Praça Onze **E** C 4
Praça Quinze **A** B 3
Pracinhas *Viaduto dos-*
E C 3
Prado Júnior *Avenida-*
C A 3
Praia do Botafogo
F C 3
Praia Vermelha **B** D 3
Prefeito Olímpo
de Melo *Rua-* **E** A I
Presidente Vargas
(Mêtro) **A** B I-2
Primeiro de Março
Rua- **A** B 2-3
Progresso *Rua-*
A D I
Providência *Morro da-*
E B 4
Prudente de Morais

Rua- **D** D 2-4

Q

Quilombo *Pedra do-*
G C I
Quilombo *Serra do-*
G C I
Quinta da Boa Vista
E C 2
Quintino do Vale
Professor *Rua-* **E** D 3

R

Ramos **G** B 3
Ramos *Rua-* **C** B-C I
Ramos Silva *Rua-*
E D 2
Rasa *Ilha-* **G** D 4
Raul Pompéia *Rua-*
C C-D I
Rebouças *Túnnel-*
D A 3
Redentor *Estrada do-*
D A I
Redonda *Ilha-* **G** D 4
Regatas Flamengo
Clube de- **D** C 2
Reinado Primeiro
Museu- **E** C 2
Remo *Estádio do-*
D C 2
República *Praça da-*
A B-C I
República do Chile
Avenida- **A** C 2
República do Peru
Rua- **C** B 2
Rezende *Rua do-*
A C I-2
Riachuelo *Rua-*
A C I-2
Ribeiro Costa General
Rua- **C** A 3
Ricardo João *Túnel-*
A B I
Ricardo Machado
Rua- **E** A I-2
Rio Branco *Avenida-*
A A-C 2-3
Rio Branco Visconde
do *Rua-* **A** C I-2
Rio Comprido **E** D 3
Rio de Janeiro
Autodromo- **G** C 2
Rio de Janeiro
Avenida- **F** A 3
Rio de Janeiro
"Galeão" *Aeroporto
Internacional do-* **G** A 3
Rivadávia Carreia
Rua- **E** A-B 4
Rocha Oliveira *Rua-*
D B 2
Rodolfo Dantas *Rua-*
C A-B 2
Rodrigo de Freitas
Lagoa- **F** C 3
Rodrigo Otávio *Rua-*
D C I
Romerio Neto
Ministro *Praça-*
D D 2
Romerio Noronha
Almirante *Avenida-*
A C-D 3-4
Rotary Internacional
Avenida- **E** B 2

Roxo Belford *Rua-*
C A 2-3
Rui Barbosa *Avenida-*
B C 2-3
Rui Barbosa *Casa-*
B C I

S

Sacadura Cabral *Rua-*
A A I
Sacarrão *Pico do-*
G C I
Sacopã *Rua-* **D** B 3-4
Sadock de Sá
Almirante *Rua-*
D C-D 3-4
Sá Ferreira *Rua-*
C C I
Sá Freire Alvim
Professor *Túnel-*
D C-D 4
Sagrada Familia *Praça-*
D B 3
Saint-Hilaire *Viaduto-*
D A-B 3
Sales Campos *Rua-*
E C-D 2
Salvador Sá *Avenida-*
E C 4
Sambaiba *Rua-* **D** D I
Sambódromo **E** C 4
San Martin General
Avenida- **D** D I-2
San Pedro-São Paulo
Viaduto- **E** B-C 4
Santa Bárbara *Ilha de-*
F A 3
Santa Bárbara *Túnel-*
B A I
Santa Casa da
Misericórdia **A** B-C 3
Santa Clara *Rua-*
C A-B I
Santa Edwiges *Praça-*
E B 3
Santa Isabel
Côrtes de- **F** B I
Santa Luzia *Rua -*
A C 3
Santana *Campo de-*
A B-C I
Santana *Rua de-* **A** C I
Santa Tereza **F** B 3
Santa Tereza
Ladeira de- **A** C-D 2
Santa Terezinha do
Menino Jesus **B** D 2
Santo Afonso *Rua-*
E D I
Santo Amaro *Rua-*
B A 2
Santo Cristo **E** B 4
Santo Cristo *Praça-*
E B 4
Santo Cristo *Rua-*
E B 4
Santos Dumont
Aeroporto- **F** B 4
Santos Dumont
Praça- **D** C I
Santos Eduardo *Rua-*
A C-D I
Santos Noronha
Praça- **E** C 4
Santos Rodrigues
Morro de- **E** D 4
São Antônio
Convento- **A** C 2

Glossary

Aqueduto : aqueduct
Avenida : avenue
Cabo : cape
Enseada : cove, inlet
Estação : station
Estrada : road
Ilha : island
Jardim : garden

Ladeira : hillside
Lagoa : lagoon
Largo : square, open public area
Morro : hill, mound
Parque : park
Pedra : mountain
Pico : peak

Pontal, ponta : headland
Ponte : bridge
Praça : square
Praia : beach
Rodovia : motorway
Rua : street
Travessa : short cut
Viaduto : viaduct

General index

See pages 6–15 for practical information about getting there, getting around, and getting by.

Index

We would like to thank Riotur, Olivier and Manuèle Colas, Lionel Roux, Xavier Pernée and all the organizations represented in this guide for their cooperation.

Picture
Credits

1 and front cover (Corcovado): ill. Donald Grant. The vignettes illustrating the various headings on the cover are taken from the inside pages of the guide and credited below.
6 Patrick Léger
8 Patrick Léger (picture 1 and picture 2 – Santos Dumont mural, aerial view); Seymourina Cruse (other pictures)
10 Seymourina Cruse (bus and taxi); Patrick Léger (other pictures)
12 Seymourina Cruse (police car); Patrick Léger (other pictures)
14 Patrick Léger ('Surf' sign); Riotur (other pictures)
16 Cæsar Park
19 Copacabana Palace / Sergio Pagano (picture 1); Méridien Copacabana (picture 3); Leme Othon Palace (picture 6)
21 Sofitel Rio Palace (picture 7); Patrick Léger (pictures 8 and 9); Rio Othon Palace (picture 10)
23 Cæsar Park (pictures 14); Arpoador Inn (picture 20)
25 Seymourina Cruse (picture 22 – view of the Novo Mundo); Patrick Léger (other pictures)
26 Manuèle Colas ('Casa 5 Lote 4' sign, and pictures 28, 30 and 34); Olivier Colas (pictures 33 and 35)
28 Roteiros de Charme (picture 36 – hotel swimming pool, picture 38 and picture 39 – entrance to hotel); Locanda della Mimosa (picture 36 – Danio and Lilian in front of the hotel); Solar da Ponte (picture 39 – hotel interior)
30 Patrick Léger
32 Seymourina Cruse (cashews and display of peppers); Patrick Léger (other pictures)
34 Patrick Léger (all pictures)
37 Patrick Léger (all pictures); logos of Antiquarius and Garcia & Rodrigues
39 Patrick Léger (all pictures)
41 Patrick Léger (all pictures); logo of Marius
43 Patrick Léger (all pictures)
45 Patrick Léger (all pictures); old postcard of the Alba Mar
47 Patrick Léger (all pictures)
48 Riotur
50 Patrick Léger (all pictures)
53 Patrick Léger (all pictures)
55 Patrick Léger (all pictures)
56 Patrick Léger
59 Patrick Léger (all pictures)
61 Riotur (Carnival costumes, Sambodrome)
62 Riotur
64 Riotur (aerial view by night, cable-car, woman in swimming costume); Patrick Léger (other pictures)
67 Riotur (picture 2 – Carmelite church and Cândido Mendes tower); Patrick Léger (other pictures)
69 Riotur / Maurice Balbino (picture 5); Riotur / Gal Oppido (picture 7); Patrick Léger (pictures 6 and 8)
71 Riotur / Gal Oppido (picture 9 – Cinelândia, picture 15 – Centro Cultural Banco do Brasil); Riotur / Maurice Balbino (picture 10 – interior of the Teatro Municipal); Patrick Léger (other pictures)
73 Riotur / Maurice Balbino (picture 18 – Burle Marx garden);

Patrick Léger (other pictures)
75 Riotur / Maurice Balbino (picture 24 – Museu da Republica); Patrick Léger (other pictures)
77 Riotur / Gal Oppido (picture 27 – The Bonde and picture 28 – Arcos da Lapa); Patrick Léger (pictures 29, 30 and 32)
79 Patrick Léger (all pictures)
81 Riotur (girl seen from behind); Riotur / Maurice Balbino (picture 43 – Grumari); Patrick Léger (other pictures)
83 Rio Convention & Visitors Bureau / Marco Aurélio Fadiga (picture 45 – Jardim Botanico, picture 50 – Parque da Cidade, red flower); Riotur (picture 47 – Vista Chinesa); Patrick Léger (other pictures)
85 Riotur (head of Christ the Redeemer, train and general view around Corcovado); Seymourina Cruse (picture 55 – Museum of Contemporary Art, Niterói); Patrick Léger (other pictures)
87 Riotur (terraces of the Maracanã); Seymourina Cruse (picture 61 –Vasco da Gama badge); Patrick Léger (other pictures)
88 Divulgação prefeitura de Angra dos Reis
90 Olivier Colas (picture 3 – house at Búzios); Manuèle Colas (picture 2 – Angra dos Reis); Patrick Léger (pictures 4 – façade and general view of Palácio Imperial; Prefeitura Municipal de Tiradentes (picture 8 – general view of Tiradentes); Xavier Pernée (picture 8 – window in Tiradentes, picture 10 – view over the roofs of Ouro Prêto); Lionel Roux (picture 11 – Mariana)
93 Olivier Colas (picture 1 – marina at Paraty and picture 3 – house at Búzios); Manuèle Colas (picture 2 – Angra dos Reis); Prefeitura Municipal de Paraty (pictures 1 – Igreja Capelinha and

Cachoeira do Griri); Anibal Seiaretta (picture 3 – Praia Azeda Lotada at Búzios)
95 Lionel Roux (picture 4 – church at Petrópolis); Patrick Léger (other pictures)
97 Prefeitura Municipal de Tiradentes (the two general views of Tiradentes); Xavier Pernée (the two windows); Katia Lombardio (church of São João del Rei)
99 Xavier Pernée (picture 10 – view of the roofs of Ouro Prêto); Lionel Roux (picture 11 – Mariana); Eduardo Tropia Cia. da Foto (picture 9 – church of São Francisco d'Assis); Belotur / Henry Yu (picture 9 – Feira de Arte e Artesanatao); Belotur / Inês Gomez (large picture 9 – Parque das Mangabeiras, Praça das Águas)
100 Seymourina Cruse
103 Patrick Léger (all pictures)
105 Patrick Léger (all pictures)
107 Patrick Léger (all pictures)
109 Borogodó (lace); Patrick Léger (other pictures)
111 Maximino (Topaz jewelry); Patrick Léger (other pictures)
112 Seymourina Cruse (cashews); Patrick Léger (other pictures)
114 Patrick Léger
117 Patrick Léger (all pictures)
119 Business Quality (man in office); Patrick Léger (other pictures)
120 Patrick Léger

Notes

Notes